The Law and the Gospel

The Law and the Gospel

Ernest C. Reisinger

P&R
PUBLISHING
P.O. BOX 817 • PHILLIPSBURG • NEW JERSEY 08865-0817

Composition by Colophon Typesetting

Printed in the United States of America

Library of Congress Cataloging-in-Publication Data

Reisinger, Ernest C., 1919–
    The law and the gospel / Ernest C. Reisinger.
      p.   cm.
    Includes bibliographical references.
    ISBN 0-87552-387-0 (pbk.)
    1. Law and gospel.   2. Ten commandments—Criticism,
interpretation, etc.   3. Law (Theology)   4. Christianity and
culture.   5. United States—Moral conditions.   6. United
States—Social conditions.   I. Title
BT79.R45   1997
241'.2—dc21   97-197

Acknowledgments
and
Appreciation

To

the wife of my youth and old age,
who did many hours of computer work;

my son, Don,
for his helpful suggestions and proofreading;

Carol Brandt,
a teacher of writing skills,
whose know-how served to strengthen
every chapter of this book.
I deeply appreciate her contribution;

Veronica Owens,
my former secretary,
for typing and retyping,
and encouragement to persevere in writing;

James Eshelman,
manager of Banner of Truth Trust, USA,
for his help and encouragement;

Robert G. den Dulk,
and the den Dulk Christian Foundation,
for their help and encouragement.

Contents

Foreword

EVERYONE LAMENTS the increasing moral decay of American society. Crime and violence have turned our homes into fortresses and given birth to security as an industry. Sexual perversion and political scandal have become such fixed parts of the American landscape that it is now the chaste young person and the honest politician who amaze us.

While preachers decry it, congressmen debate our culture's moral degeneration, and taxpayers pay for it, few people have zeroed in on the real reason for it. God is the Creator. He has made humanity for Himself. He has given to men and women a fixed moral code, a standard by which we must live. Romans 1 teaches us that where this standard is expelled, God's judgment soon replaces it. What is taking place in our culture will never be properly assessed until it is seen in the light of God's absolute, unchanging moral standard.

Without a renewed emphasis on God's law, our nation will remain like a ship at sea without a rudder; like a man lost in the wilderness without a compass. Christians, above all people, must be clear on this point. The volume you now hold in your hand provides sound, biblical thinking on this issue.

Ernest Reisinger goes big-game hunting in this book. Lesser issues are put aside while he sets his sights on the very heart of biblical Christianity. Few subjects compare in importance with "law and gospel." It is the hub from which all other biblical doctrines extend. To be unclear on either law or gospel is to be spiritually paralyzed. To confuse the relationship between the two is to fall into serious, crippling error.

Whether or not one agrees with the arguments set forth in this book, an honest reader will be forced to conclude that the subject is vitally important to a proper understanding of God's Word. All of the Bible is either law or gospel. God, man, sin, Christ, redemption, grace, guilt, judgment, atonement, forgiveness, and holiness are all revealed to us in the Scriptures in terms of law and gospel. The Christian who neglects the study of this subject, therefore, does so to his own spiritual detriment.

As important as the subject is, it has been tragically neglected by modern Bible-believing Christians. The present generation of evangelicals simply assumes that it understands the gospel. Yet, as several recent studies have embarrassingly revealed, a majority cannot even cite the basic content of the gospel. Fortunately, this easy peace with a contentless Christianity is being increasingly challenged by respected evangelical leaders.

But a necessary component of the renaissance of God's gospel must be the rediscovery of God's law. In fact, the gospel cannot be established on any other foundation than that of law. This was readily acknowledged by earlier generations of Christians. Prior to this century sermons and studies on the Ten Commandments were commonplace in Bible-believing churches. Today, not only have the commandments been expelled from our schools and our courthouses, they have effectively been discarded in our churches. Less than 1 percent of all church members can even recite the Ten Commandments!

The failure to teach God's law in our churches has had devastating consequences. Not only is gross sin being flaunted in the public square, but also the moral conduct of our church children has degenerated to alarming proportions. Josh McDowell has recently published the results of his study of young people actively involved in evangelical churches. He discovered that within the previous three months,

- 66 percent had lied to their parents,
- 36 percent had cheated on their exams,

- 55 percent had engaged in sexual activity,
- 20 percent had tried to hurt someone physically.

Most of these teenagers profess to believe the gospel for salvation. Yet, most are not obeying God's law. Something is gravely wrong.

The relationship between law and gospel desperately needs to be rediscovered in our day. The law was given to teach sinners their sin. When a sinner sees the law in all its strictness and spirituality, he thereby comes to understand the spiritual bankruptcy and grave danger of his condition. The law, able to condemn but unable to save, sends the convicted sinner looking for salvation in the only place it can be found. It sends him to Jesus Christ who, in His perfect law-fulfilling life and perfect law-fulfilling death, gave Himself to redeem helpless sinners.

When Christ receives repentant, believing men and women, He forgives them, grants them His righteousness, and gives them His Spirit. He writes His law on their new hearts and empowers them to follow Him in obedient discipleship. As the One who perfectly kept the law Himself, He then leads His disciples to obey the commandments.

The spirit of our present age insists that relativism is the only truth, and tolerance is the only virtue. Absolutes are seen as archaic, and right and wrong are forgotten categories.

The church, rather than effectively standing against this spirit, has been infected by it. We have lost our moorings. We have forsaken our foundations. Until they are recovered, God's people will lack the spiritual ability and moral authority to resist the onslaught of cultural decadence.

I KNOW VERY FEW PEOPLE who are qualified to write such a book as this. Biblical, theological, and historical understanding of the issues is essential. Anyone expounding the great themes related to law and gospel faces perils on both the right hand and the left. It is not easy to avoid the Scylla of legalism and the Charybdis of antinomianism. History bears sad testimony to this fact.

Ernest Reisinger charts a trustworthy and rewarding course through that narrow passage. He does so not as some unbiased, uninvolved observer, but rather as a fellow pilgrim, a pastor and a teacher in the church of Jesus Christ. His passion for the subject comes through on every page. His familiar discourse with spiritual giants of previous generations is also evident. What he has written here is in harmony with the great creeds, confessions, and catechisms that grew out of the Protestant Reformation.

Though the insights that follow may strike many readers as new thoughts, be assured that there is nothing novel about them. They are an exposition of that faith which has been once for all delivered to the saints. This book not only should be read but should be studied diligently by every child of God who has any interest in seeing biblical Christianity flourish in our churches once again.

—THOMAS ASCOL

Introduction

"He will magnify the law and make it honorable." (Isa. 42:21)

TWO STATEMENTS MADE IN MY HEARING have had a profound influence on me, giving me an insatiable desire to know the relationship between the Ten Commandments (the moral law) and the gospel of Christ. They have to do with the proper connection between law and gospel, how each is meant to serve and establish the other. (Historically our Christian fathers, as well as the great creeds and confessions of the faith, have referred to the Ten Commandments as the "moral law." I will often do likewise.)

One statement was from an old Southern Baptist evangelist who has since gone on to his reward. He said, "The first message of the cross is the law of God."

The other statement came from the late Professor John Murray, who related to me the following story: He was visiting his closest ministerial friend in Canada, a very reserved man who never raised his voice in the pulpit. On this particular communion Sunday, however, when the normally quiet minister came down from the pulpit to stand by the communion table, he raised his hands in ecstasy and cried out, "O Calvary, whose base is eternal justice and whose spirit is eternal love."

After many years of seeking to understand the relationship between the law and the gospel, I have come to understand just how profound these two statements were.

As I approach the topic of the law and the gospel, the words of Elihu found in Job 32:18–19 best describe my feeling: "I am full of words; the spirit within me compels me. Indeed my belly

is like wine that has no vent; it is ready to burst like new wine-
skins." I have before me forty manila folders full of notes and
excerpts from many books, confessions, catechisms, and com-
mentaries. I am indeed "ready to burst."

I claim no original thinking for the ideas in these studies but
have received help from these and other sources—some acknowledged and some not. I believe the material set forth here
to be true biblical teaching. The positions expressed fall within
the framework of the teaching summarized in the great historic
creeds of the church, such as The Heidelberg Catechism, The
Westminster Confession, and The Old Baptist Confession of
1689 (London Confession). There is nothing novel here, and the
insights in this book may be used by others without credit.

My motives for these studies on the law and the gospel are
to promote conviction of sin and misery in the conscience of the
unconverted and true holiness in the heart and life of the Christian. It will be my constant endeavor to render this subject easy
and intelligible to serious and devout readers. These studies are
meant not for theological giraffes but for ordinary sheep in
God's flock who sincerely hunger for the truth.

My principal method will be to convince the reader's mind,
not to irritate the emotions, lest while seeking to serve grace, I
promote sin, or endeavoring to lead men and women to holiness, I stir up their corruptions. I will seek to address principles,
not attack persons.

It is my earnest desire that what is here plain to the eye, the
God of truth will make evident to the heart—that He would
give the reader sound spiritual judgment. It is also my unfeigned desire that this feeble attempt to promote true faith
and holiness may obtain the approval of our matchless Redeemer, and, by His blessing, be used for the glorious cause of
evangelical truth in the world.

Law and Gospel: Distinct yet Inseparable

To blend or confound the law and the gospel has been a fatal
source of error and division in the Christian church, and has

embarrassed many believers not a little in their exercise of faith and practice of holiness. Charles Haddon Spurgeon, that great preacher and soul winner, said, "There is no point upon which men make greater mistakes than upon the relationship which exists between the law and the gospel" (*The New Park Street Pulpit* [Grand Rapids: Zondervan, 1963], 1:285). In another sermon entitled *"The Perpetuity of the Law of God"* he stated, "The man who knows the relative position of the law and the gospel has the keys of the situation in the matter of doctrine" (*The Metropolitan Tabernacle* [Edinburgh: Banner of Truth, 1971], 28:277).

There can be no true evangelical holiness, of either heart or life, unless it proceeds from faith working by love; and no true faith, of either the law or the gospel, unless the main distinction between the one and the other is spiritually discerned. The law and the gospel are set before us in the Bible as one undivided system of truth; yet an unchangeable line of distinction is drawn between them. There is also an inseparable connection and relationship between them.

Many leaders of the past have acknowledged both this distinction and relationship. J. Gresham Machen, the great Princetonian and principal founder of Westminster Theological Seminary, wrote,

> A new and more powerful proclamation of that law is perhaps the most pressing need of the hour; men would have little difficulty with the gospel if they had only learned the lesson of the law. . . . So it always is: a low view of the law always brings legalism in religion; a high view of law makes a man a seeker after grace. Pray God that the high view may again prevail. (*What Is Faith?* [Edinburgh: Banner of Truth, 1946], 141–42)

The great apostle Paul put it succinctly: "Do we then make void the law through faith? Certainly not! On the contrary, we establish the law" (Rom. 3:31).

Charles Bridges has noted,

The mark of a minister "approved unto God, a workman that needeth not to be ashamed," is, that he "rightly
divides the word of truth." This implies a full and direct application of the gospel to the mass of his unconverted hearers, combined with a body of spiritual instruction to the several classes of Christians. His system
will be marked by Scriptural symmetry and compre-
hensiveness. It will embrace the whole revelation of
God, in its doctrinal instructions, experimental privileges and practical results. This revelation is divided
into two parts—the Law and the Gospel—essentially
distinct from each other; though so intimately connected, that no accurate knowledge of either can be obtained without the other. . . . (*The Christian Ministry*
[London: Banner of Truth, 1967], 222)

The law, like Christ, has always been crucified between two
thieves—antinomianism on the one side and legalism on the
other. The antinomian sees no relationship between the law
and the gospel except that of being set free. The legalist fails to
understand that vital distinction between the two.

Some preach the law instead of the gospel. Some modify
them and preach neither the law nor the gospel. Some think the
law is the gospel, and some think the gospel is the law; those
who hold these views are not clear on either.

But others ask: Has not the law been fully abrogated by the
coming of Christ into the world? Would you bring us under that
heavy yoke of bondage which no one has ever been able to
bear? Does not the New Testament expressly declare that we
are not under the law but under grace? That Christ was made
under the law to free His people from it? Is not an attempt to
over-awe men's conscience by the authority of the Decalogue
a legalistic imposition, altogether at variance with the Christian
liberty the Savior has brought us by His obedience unto death?

We answer: Far from the law's being abolished by the coming of Christ into this world, He Himself emphatically stated,
"Do not think that I came to destroy the Law or the Prophets

[or the enforcers thereof]. I did not come to destroy but to fulfill. For assuredly, I say to you, till heaven and earth pass away, one jot or one tittle will by no means pass from the law till all is fulfilled" (Matt. 5:17–18). True, the Christian is not under the law as a covenant of works, nor as a ministration of condemnation, but he is under it as a *rule of life and an objective standard of righteousness for all people for all times.*

Our Need for a Rule of Life

The power of a holy life needs to be accompanied by instruction in the pattern of holiness. In what does sanctified behavior consist? It consists in pleasing God. What is it that pleases God? Doing His will. Where is His will to be discerned? In His holy law. The law, then, is the Christian's rule of life, and the believer finds that he delights in the law of God after the inward man (Rom. 7:22). The Christian is not lawless but "under the law to Christ," a phrase from Paul that would be more accurately rendered "in the law to Christ" (1 Cor. 9:21). Sin is lawlessness, and salvation is the bringing of the lawless one into his true relation to God, within the blessedness of His holy law. The law of Moses is not other than the law of Christ; it is an objective standard just as Christ is our pattern.

The Ten Commandments were uniquely honored by God, founded in love, and they are obeyed out of affection for the One who provided redemption. A. W. Pink wrote concerning the Ten Commandments,

> Their uniqueness appears first in that this revelation of God at Sinai—which was to serve for all coming ages as the grand expression of His holiness and the summation of man's duty—was attended with such awe-inspiring phenomena that the very manner of their publication plainly showed that God Himself assigned to the Decalogue peculiar importance. The Ten Commandments were uttered by God in an audible voice, with the fearful adjuncts of clouds and darkness, thunders and light-

nings and the sound of a trumpet, and they were the only parts of Divine Revelation so spoken—none of the ceremonial or civil precepts were thus distinguished. Those Ten Words, and they alone, were written by the finger of God upon tables of stone, and they alone were deposited in the holy ark for safe keeping. Thus, in the unique honor conferred upon the Decalogue itself we may perceive its paramount importance in the Divine government. (*The Ten Commandments* [Swengel, Pa.: Reiner, 1961], 5)

The moral law carries permanent validity because it is an objective standard uniquely sanctioned by God and goes straight to the root of our modern problems. It lays its finger on the church's deepest need in evangelism as well as in the Christian life: sanctification. The Ten Commandments are desperately needed not only in the church but also in society. We live in a lawless age at the end of the twentieth century. Lawlessness reigns in the home, in the church, in the school, and in the land. The Scriptures tell us that "righteousness exalts a nation, but sin is a reproach to any people."

The law restrains sin. Without the moral law this world would be a field of blood, as is evidenced in places where there is no regard for God's commands. The Puritan, Samuel Bolton, in *The True Bounds of Christian Freedom* ([London: Banner of Truth, 1964], 79), explained,

> Blessed be God that there is this fear upon the spirits of wicked men; otherwise we could not well live in the world. One man would be a devil to another. Every man would be a Cain to his brother, an Amon to his sister, an Absolom to his father, a Saul to himself, a Judas to his master; for what one does, all men would do, were it not for a restraint upon their spirits.

Tragically, Christians have contributed to our society's moral decline by removing the Ten Commandments from their instruction.

Not only the wicked, but also followers of God need an objective, fixed, absolute standard of right and wrong. A devotional life cannot exist without regard to morality. We cannot separate devotion from duty. After all, what constitutes a devout person? Someone who is seeking to do the will of God, someone who is instructed in sanctified behavior. And, again, in what does that behavior consist? In doing the will of God as summarized in the Ten Commandments.

The subject of these studies, law and gospel, is most important both to saints and to sinners. To know experientially the relationship between them is to "be wise unto salvation." To live habitually in that knowledge is to be at once holy and happy. It will keep one from verging toward self-righteousness, on the one hand, and licentiousness, on the other. A clear and distinct understanding of the law and the gospel enables one to assert both the absolute freeness of sovereign grace and the sacred interests of true holiness. Without a living knowledge and an unfeigned faith of the law and the gospel, a person can neither venerate the authority of the one nor esteem the grace of the other.

Law and Gospel: Central to the Whole Bible

The law and the gospel are the principal parts of divine revelation; or rather, they are the center, the sum, and the substance of the whole. Every passage of sacred Scripture is either law or gospel. Even the histories of the Old and New Testaments, as far as the agency of man is introduced, are but narratives of acts done in conformity or opposition to the moral law, and done in the belief or disbelief of the gospel. The ordinances of the ceremonial law, given to the ancient Israelites, were for the most part grafted on the second and fourth commandments of the moral law, and as types, were an obscure revelation of the gospel. The precepts of the judicial law are all reducible to commandments of the moral law, especially to those of the second table. All warnings, whether in the Old Testament or in the New, are warnings either of the law or of the gospel. Every promise is either of the one or of the other. Every prophecy of

Scripture is a declaration of things obscure, or future, connected either with the law or the gospel, or with both. And there is not one admonition, reproof, or exhortation in the sacred volume, but what refers to either the law or the gospel, or both.

If then a man cannot distinguish the law from the gospel, he cannot rightly understand so much as a single article of divine truth. If he does not have spiritual and just apprehensions of the holy law, he cannot have spiritual and transforming discoveries of the glorious gospel. And if his views of the gospel are wrong, his notions of the law cannot be right.

Besides, if the speculative knowledge that true believers themselves have of the law and the gospel are superficial and indistinct, they will often be in danger of mingling the one with the other and they will, in a greater degree than can be conceived, retard their progress in holiness, as well as in peace and comfort. But if they can distinguish well between the law and the gospel, they will thereby, under the illuminating influences of the Holy Spirit, be able (1) to discern the glory of the whole scheme of redemption, (2) to reconcile all passages of Scripture that appear contrary to each other, (3) to try doctrines as to whether they are of God, (4) to calm their own consciences in times of mental trouble, and (5) to advance resolutely in evangelical holiness and spiritual consolation.

Thus the law and the gospel are the center, the sum, and the substance of the whole Bible. How important then is it to properly relate and distinguish the two? The closer we get to a clear view of the difference between the law and the gospel and the connection between them as they serve to establish each other, the more we will understand the Holy Scriptures and thus the will and mind of God, and the more useful we will be in His service.

Charles Spurgeon, in a sermon on Romans 5:20 (*New Park Street Pulpit*, sermon 37 [Grand Rapids: Zondervan], 1:286), declared,

> There is no point of biblical interpretation and application where men make greater mistakes than the rela-

tionship which exists between the Law and the Gospel. . . . some put Law instead of the Gospel, some modify the Law and the Gospel and therefore preach neither Law nor Gospel.

If men blend the Law with the Gospel or Faith with Works (which is the same thing), especially in the area of Justification, they will obscure the glory of redeeming grace and prevent themselves and others from having the real joy and peace in believing. They will also retard their progress in holiness.

Ah! but if men, under the influence of the Holy Spirit, are able to see the glory of the whole plan of Redemption—if they are able to reconcile the passages of Scripture which seem contrary to each other (and there are some) they would advance in true holiness and spiritual consolation.

To see the glory of the whole would be a means to calm the conscience in times of mental and spiritual trouble. You see, a troubled conscience cannot be properly quieted unless the Gospel is rightly distinguished from the Law; on the other hand, there will be no troubled conscience to be quieted without the Law.

In order, then, to help the devout reader distinguish between the law and the gospel so as to realize those inexpressibly important objectives, I shall, in humble dependence on the Spirit of truth, consider some relevant questions.

Some Questions Before Us

1. Do those under grace have a duty to keep the Ten Commandments as a rule of life?
2. Does the gospel of Christ abrogate the Ten Commandments?
3. Does the law have any role in the work of evangelism?
4. What is the difference between the moral, the ceremonial, and the civil law?

5. What is the proper relationship between God's law and God's love?
6. What are some of the rules or principles for a right understanding of the commandments?
7. What is the relationship between Moses and Christ?
8. What is the relationship between the law and the Savior?
9. What is the relationship between the law and grace?
10. What is the gospel and its relationship to the law?

It will be proper to consider the difference between the law and the gospel as well as the agreement between them. The establishment of the law by the gospel, or the subservience of the gospel to the authority and honor of the law, will be addressed. The believer's privilege of being dead to the law as a covenant of works, and the necessary consequences will also be a topic.

I do not wish to be unduly polemical. I am more anxious to set out and establish what I conceive to be the truth than to dissect the minute and laborious details of the false. For this reason I have omitted personal references to recent advocates of other current views, except where necessary.

GOD SPOKE ALL THESE WORDS, SAYING:

"I am the LORD your God, who brought you out of the land of Egypt, out of the house of bondage.

You shall have no other gods before Me.

You shall not make for yourself any carved image, or any likeness of anything that is in heaven above, or that is in the earth beneath, or that is in the water under the earth; you shall not bow down to them nor serve them. For I, the LORD your God, am a jealous God, visiting the iniquity of the fathers on the children to the third and fourth generations of those who hate Me, but showing mercy to thousands, to those who love Me and keep My commandments.

You shall not take the name of the LORD your God in vain, for the LORD will not hold him guiltless who takes His name in vain.

Remember the Sabbath day, to keep it holy. Six days you shall labor and do all your work, but the seventh day is the Sabbath of the LORD your God. In it you shall do no work: you, nor your son, nor your daughter, nor your manservant, nor your maidservant, nor your cattle, nor your stranger who is within your gates. For in six days the LORD made the heavens and earth, the sea, and all that is in them, and rested the seventh day. Therefore the LORD blessed the Sabbath day, and hallowed it.

Honor your father and your mother, that your days may be long upon the land which the LORD your God is giving you.

You shall not murder.

You shall not commit adultery.

You shall not steal.

You shall not bear false witness against your neighbor.

You shall not covet your neighbor's house; you shall not covet your neighbor's wife, nor his manservant, nor his maidservant, nor his ox, nor his donkey, nor anything that is your neighbor's."
(Ex. 20:1–17; see also Deut. 5:6-21)

CHAPTER ONE

Values Gone Awry

*". . . their foolish hearts were
darkened." (Rom. 1:21)*

WE HEAR A LOT ABOUT "FAMILY VALUES": from politicians, Hollywood, talk shows, and the news media. But do people know what "family values" are, particularly with respect to moral standards?

The Dark Side of "Family Values"

Bonnie Lynn Matthews and Elaine Kohler, recently pictured in the *Florida News-Press*, are admitted lesbians, living together, and are suing the state for taking a six-year-old child from them. They want to become foster parents. "He is our kid, we are his moms [plural]," they say. Both are mental health counselors. Kohler is an "in-home" therapist to foster children. Matthews is a therapist for emotionally disturbed and abused children. They have their own idea of "family values."

So does Murphy Brown. But her values exclude the seventh commandment. Likewise, homosexual men who marry men and want to adopt children also have "family values," but they deny any fixed, objective, absolute standard of right and wrong. And what about sports heroes who get AIDS through sexual immorality? They become heroes and are treated as role models of domestic virtue.

1

Woody Allen has his own version of "family values." He made the cover of *Time* for what the magazine called his "unconventional family," in which he had an affair with the adopted daughter of his paramour. *Time* quoted Allen as saying that he saw no moral dilemma in having an affair with Mia Farrow's child. If having sex with Farrow is acceptable, who is to say it is wrong to have sex with Farrow's daughter?

What sort of "family values" does the Duchess of York, Sarah Fergeson, have? She was photographed topless with a man not her husband—while her children looked on. That is "family values" of the wrong kind!

In the seventh commandment, God almighty condemns such behavior regardless of what it is called. "Woe to those who call evil good; and good evil; who put darkness for light and light for darkness" (Isa. 5:20). The Lord has given us a fixed, objective, perfect, eternal standard of right and wrong, and it does not square with just any definition of the family and its values. But our society is rapidly falling away from that standard. We may have won the cold war against communism and the short war in the Persian Gulf, but we are losing the moral war in the home, the school, and the church. Why? We no longer hold to an absolute criterion of right and wrong.

For fifty years our educational system has consciously or unconsciously been pressing for an amoral society by teaching that all morals are relative. How can any politician, Republican or Democrat, push for "family values" without a fixed, objective standard of righteousness? It is folly to think we can engender character in men and women by taking away from them their duty and responsibility to the Creator of all the earth, who will judge the world in righteousness. God has given us His definition of "family values." They are the values summarized in the Ten Commandments.

God Gave Them Up

Immorality is promoted not only in public schools and universities but through the entertainment media. Movies and television romanticize macho violence and naked women. Rock concerts and rap music stir up raw lust and violence. Pornography is all over the magazine racks.

Social programs and rehab centers do some good in curtailing certain vices, but they cannot touch the root of the problem. Programs will not transform evil men and evil women into good men and good women. Why? They do not reach the heart. They are not spiritual. They do not have the right moral standard. They are disconnected from the principles and power of the Creator God.

The Bible offers this explanation of the moral crisis we are experiencing today:

> Although they knew God, they did not glorify Him as God, nor were thankful, but became futile in their thoughts, and their foolish hearts were darkened. Professing to be wise, they became fools, and changed the glory of the incorruptible God into an image made like corruptible man—and birds and four-footed beasts and creeping things. Therefore God also gave them up to uncleanness, in the lusts of their hearts, to dishonor their bodies among themselves, who exchanged the truth of God for the lie, and worshiped and served the creature rather than the Creator, who is blessed forever. Amen. For this reason God gave them up to vile passions. For even their women exchanged the natural use for what is against nature. Likewise also the men, leaving the natural use of the woman, burned in their lust for one another, men with men committing what is shameful, and receiving in themselves the penalty of their error which was due. And even as they did not like to retain God in their knowledge, God gave them over to a debased mind, to do those things which are not fitting. . . . (Rom. 1:21–28)

Paul's words sound like a summary of the daily news. We could give them the heading, "What Happens When a Privi-

leged Society Abandons God?" The answer is found in verses
24, 26, and 28—*God abandons that society.*

- "Therefore God gave them up" (v. 24).
- "For this cause God gave them up" (v. 26).
- "God gave them over" (v. 28).

In this passage, we find mass apostasy as people turn from
the worship of the invisible, true, and living God and embrace
grotesque idolatry. No other Scripture addresses our present society more pointedly. Here the great apostle teaches us what
happens when a privileged society such as ours abandons God.
In a solemn act of judgment, God abandoned the people described in Romans 1. If He gave that sinful people over to its
own corruption, should we be surprised if He sends judgment
on us? Surely AIDS is the judgment of God, but it is minute
compared to the judgment mentioned in verses 24, 26, and 28.
God abandoned them. He did not make them sinful; He merely
removed the restraints. But when God gives a society over to
its own lusts and corruption, that society is under the most
awesome and terrible judgment that can come upon any people, short of hell itself.

Marks of an Abandoned Society

When a privileged society abandons God, three things emerge,
all of which are very evident today: (1) There is *rampant sexual
perversion.* A great deal of this passage in Romans has to do with
the sexual perversions that characterized the Gentiles in Paul's
day.

A few things need to be said about human sexuality: (a) Sexuality is a God-given reality. God made men and women sexual beings. (b) Sexuality is one of the strongest forces within a
normal human being. It is necessary for the continuance of the
human race according to God's purpose. The first command in
the Bible, is to "be fruitful and multiply" (Gen. 1:28). You cannot do that without sex. (c) Because human sexuality is God-

given, it is nothing to be ashamed of or embarrassed about when it is enjoyed within the God-given bonds of marriage. But because of the power and force of sexuality, nothing has been more corrupted and abused by sinful men and women. Whenever people have abandoned the revealed truth of God concerning sexuality, perversion and shame have been the inevitable results.

(2) A related mark of an abandoned society is *homosexuality and lesbianism,* which are clearly an abomination in the sight of God. Nevertheless, groups within our present-day society are putting forth intense efforts to make such lifestyles acceptable. There are serious efforts to change social attitudes toward homosexuality. The homosexual lobby is well organized and powerful enough to succeed in its appeals for tolerance, all the while showing intolerance of those who believe as a matter of principle that homosexuality is wrong. Christians should make their convictions known with clarity, kindness, and compassion.

(3) A third mark of an abandoned society is *social breakdown.* That is because you cannot divorce morality from true religion, which is first of all a relationship with God. In Western civilization, our laws and our way of life on the whole have arisen out of the teaching of the Bible. Many people lament the increase in crime, the decline of law and order, and the break-up of the family without recognizing that these painful realities result directly from our society's rejection of biblical morality found in the Ten Commandments. Is it not obvious that the common good and countless blessings flow from walking with God according to His commands? Imagine what it would be like if everyone obeyed the commandments; if every one loved God and his neighbor as himself; if all children obeyed their parents; if no one took the Lord's name in vain, or stole, or murdered, or committed adultery, or lied; if no one coveted his neighbor's house, his wife, or his possessions. It would be wonderful—it would be perfect—it would be heaven! The Ten Commandments are for our good as well as God's glory. But a society that abandons God's law, also abandons the blessings of His presence.

My point is not that law keeping is the way of salvation.
There is only one way to be saved, and it is not by keeping the
commandments but by believing on the Lord Jesus Christ. He
is the Way, the Truth, and the Life. But He calls all humanity to
obedience. And there is a general connection between the extent to which a society as a whole obeys God's absolute moral
standard and the degree to which they enjoy His blessings.
There is no other true standard of right and wrong, and therefore there is no other way to live.

Even among the unconverted, the law has the positive role
of restricting evil and convicting hearts so that sinners turn to
Christ for salvation. Without the moral law, there is no awareness of sin. "For by the law is the knowledge of sin" (Rom. 3:20).
If there is no law, there is no sin, for "sin is the transgression of
the law" (1 John 3:4 KJV). Paul said, "I would not have known
sin, except through the law" (Rom. 7:7). The man who does not
know the nature of the law cannot know the nature of sin. And
he who does not know the nature of sin cannot know the nature of the Savior.

The cross makes no sense apart from the law. The cross without the law is like a jig-saw puzzle with the key piece missing.
The evangelical prophet Isaiah said, "He [Christ] will magnify
the law and make it honorable" (Isa. 42:21). Christ magnified
the law by His perfect life and in His death on the cross.

Three Responses to the Law

As we look out over our society, we can notice three kinds of
response to the Ten Commandments. There are, of course, many
shades of difference within these three responses, but all people will fall into these three general categories:

1. Those Who Ignore and Despise the Law
I need not say much about this group. Just look around in our
society, read your newspaper, or watch your television. This
group has neither the time nor the inclination to consider the
law. Many people have no scruples because they have no regard

for God's law. In the past their conscience may have accused them because the law was written on their hearts; "for when Gentiles, who do not have the law, by nature do the things contained in the law, these, although not having the law, are a law to themselves, who show the work of the law written in their hearts, their conscience also bearing witness, and between themselves their thoughts accusing or else excusing them" (Rom. 2:14–15). Now their conscience excuses them. Some are already reprobate. Such people are described in Romans 1:24, 26, and 28.

2. The Half-hearted Rationalizers

The "half-hearted" are those who compromise and rationalize their violation of the Ten Commandments. This group represents the largest part of unregenerate church members. By their unholy living, they deal the most serious blow to true religion.

Having despaired of ever obtaining personal, perfect, and perpetual obedience, the half-hearted have drawn up their own moral code, a less stringent line of conduct that will not offend their conscience. They have set their own standard, selecting only the commandments they consider important.

Though they would not murder, they may think nothing of breaking the ninth commandment and lying. They would not steal goods off the store shelf, but they may have no regard for the fourth commandment. Many think nothing of breaking the third commandment; they take the Lord's name in vain without blushing.

They habitually look for ways to soothe their conscience. For example, they may argue that it is simplistic to divide mankind into two classes, the righteous and the wicked. So they invent a third class, those who are not good enough for heaven and not bad enough for hell. And, of course, they place themselves in this category. Such compromise has always been, and always will be, a serious enemy of true religion.

Another tactic of these compromisers is the claim that Christianity cannot be defined. Or else they define it so broadly that it really means nothing. Always finding ways to elude, duck, twist, and wrest the law's stern demands, they never come to see the cross and its true meaning. Unless you see the law in its true meaning, you cannot see the true meaning of the gospel.

Half-hearted compromisers often try to offset their sins and inconsistencies by formal prayers and other religious acts, such as tithing. Oh, they are not like the first group, who ignore religion. They are not openly profane. They are religious. But they have their own standard, their own moral code. The truth of the matter is that *they have their own god!* They have crafted him in their own mind. Though they will tell you that they want to do right, they also want to *decide what is right!*

One thing is certain—theirs is not the God who reveals Himself in the Bible. They have not examined themselves by His holy, just, good, and perfect law. They have never felt their misery and, therefore, never savingly felt His mercy in the person and work of His dear Son.

3. *Those Who Know That the Law Is Holy, Just, and Good*
The third group knows that God's holy law is good and benefits all people. They know that the law comes from an all-wise and an all-loving heavenly Father. They are disappointed and dissatisfied with themselves, not with the law.

Before his conversion, Paul may not have been a murderer, a thief, or an adulterer. Outwardly he loved and worshiped God. But, oh, that tenth commandment, "You shall not covet." He discovered that the commandments are spiritual and that they go to the heart. He learned that true religion is inward. He learned about indwelling sin (Rom. 7:7). All this was made known to him through the tenth commandment. He discovered that sin lay in his nature, not only in outward acts. The outward acts of sin are a result of an inward problem—"in me [there] dwelleth no good thing" (Rom. 7:18 KJV). It was this discovery of sin by the law that turned Paul's eyes to the law-keeping Savior, and the truth that his only hope for salvation was in the person and work of this blessed, indispensable Savior. He learned that salvation is in Christ. Thus the law was his friend. It pointed him to the cross, where that condemning law was sat-

isfied for sinners. Now the bloody cross made sense to him—
it was his only hope.

After his conversion, Paul could say what Augustine would
later say: "With thy calling and thy shouting thou didst break
my deafness, with thy flashing and shining thou didst scatter
my blindness, at the scent of thee, I drew in breath and I pant
for thee. I have tasted and I hunger and thirst, thou hast touched
me and I am on fire for thy peace" (*Confessions* 10.27.28).

Those who glory in the law can say with Paul after his conversion, "I delight in the law of God according to the inward
man" (Rom. 7:22). They can exclaim with David, "O how love
I thy law! It is my meditation all the day" (Ps. 119:97 KJV). They
can prove the words of Joshua, "This Book of the Law shall not
depart from your mouth; but you shall meditate in it day and
night, that you may observe to do according to all that is written in it. For then you will make your way prosperous, and then
you will have good success" (Josh. 1:8). I pray that you, my dear
reader, are found in this third group of people.

As you face our Creator's holy, just, and good law, you have
one of three alternatives:

1. Apostasy: Turning away from God and religion; total
   desertion of the principles of the faith.
2. Hypocrisy: Picking, choosing, and rationalizing; the
   way of the large majority of modern-day church members. They have their own law and their own god, but
   not the God of the Ten Commandments.
3. Sainthood: Feeling guilt and misery by the law, and
   therefore finding grace and mercy at the cross. There is
   mercy with the Lord.

Do you see the folly of thinking that we can develop character in men, women, and children by taking away their responsibility to their Creator and their fellowmen? To violate
moral standards while acknowledging their authority is one
thing; to lose all sense of their moral claim and to repudiate all
moral authority is something far more serious and threatening.

We must disagree sharply with those liberal theologians—whether Catholic, Jew, or Protestant—who hold that our contemporary society is evolving to a "new morality" based on "love" for others rather than on the fixed, absolute, objective standards of righteousness set out in the Ten Commandments. The contemporary scene shows in fact a rejection of all moral restraints in favor of a self-indulgent quest for pleasure. Far from evolving to a higher morality, people are simply interested in getting their "kicks," by whatever means.

The distinction between right and wrong, good and evil, decent and indecent has not merely collapsed but become irrelevant. The trend toward regarding truth as relative and conditional, rather than absolute and eternal, reaches its logical conclusion in lawlessness. What can we expect when long ago the Ten Commandments were expelled from our public schools, many of our homes, and even our churches? No human ethic is possible unless it is grounded in the great Creator and His moral mandates to all creatures.

I WANT TO END THIS CHAPTER with a word of encouragement. Romans 1 is a vivid picture of our current moral climate. It is sad and depressing. But in contrast to this dark, gloomy moral forecast, I want to sound a strong note of hope.

Some of us have loved ones and friends who are caught up in the immoral lifestyles we have been talking about. There is hope for them in 1 Corinthians 6:9–11.

> Do you not know that the unrighteous will not inherit the kingdom of God? Do not be deceived. Neither fornicators, nor idolaters, nor adulterers, nor homosexuals, nor sodomites, nor thieves, nor covetous, nor drunkards, nor revilers, nor extortioners will inherit the kingdom of God. *And such were some of you. But* you were washed, but you were sanctified, but you were justified in the name of the Lord Jesus and by the Spirit of God.

It may seem odd to say that there is hope in a passage that begins with the judgment of God against lawbreakers. Yet Paul continues, "And such *were* some of you." Then comes one of the most encouraging, wonderful words in all the Bible, mentioned three times in verse 11—*"But."* The message is that the unrighteous can be changed: *"But* you were washed, *but* you were sanctified, *but* you were justified." And therein lies the hope for lawbreakers. *There is hope*—as long as someone is willing to proclaim the law and the gospel.

CHAPTER TWO

In the Beginning

*". . . who show the work of the law written in
their hearts, their conscience also bearing
witness." (Rom. 2:15)*

The Law Written on the Heart

God wrote the law on Adam's heart so that he would know
right from wrong, good from evil. The law written on the heart
is often referred to by the great church fathers and respected
theologians as the "law of creation" or "the law of nature." It
was a divine obligation impressed upon Adam's conscience
from the beginning by the almighty Creator.

As Creator, God has the right to command His creatures and
establish the terms of the relationship between them and Him.
Until creatures come to understand God's original design for
the Creator-creature relationship and the awful breach in that
relationship because of their sin, they will never be interested
in a Redeemer-redeemed relationship.

The law of nature (or of creation), continues to be impressed
upon the human mind by God apart from any tradition or instruction. There is no mortal who does not feel its force to some
degree: "What may be known of God is manifest in them, for
God has shown it to them" (Rom. 1:19). Even the Gentiles, without having received the law of Moses, are said to do by nature
the things contained in the law (Rom. 2:14). As J. B. Phillips has

paraphrased it, "When the gentiles, who have no knowledge of the Law, act in accordance with it by the light of nature, they show that they have a law in themselves."

The law inscribed on the heart cannot be read the same way one reads a book. With physical eyes we can read the Ten Commandments in Exodus 20, but we cannot read the same law written on the heart. The teaching of Hebrews 8:10 and 10:16 is that God plants in the renewed heart an affinity with and love for His law, resulting in cheerful, loving obedience. As Paul expressed it, "I joyfully concur with the law of God" (Rom. 7:22 NASB). John adds, "For this is the love of God, that we keep His commandments. And His commandments are not burdensome" (1 John 5:3).

If fallen man has the law written on his heart so that he does by nature the things of the law (Rom. 2:14), imagine how much clearer it was written on Adam's heart in his original state. And, if the renewed man has the law written upon his heart (Heb. 8:10; 10:16), surely it cannot be different in principle from what was first impressed on the heart of Adam at creation or what the Lord wrote on the tables of stone at Sinai. And so, even though the law inscribed on the heart is not as openly expressed as the fuller revelation of the law to Moses, it was in perfect agreement with it from the start.

A Test of Obedience and Complete Loyalty

The prohibition against eating from the Tree of the Knowledge of Good and Evil was the ultimate test of obedience and loyalty to the Creator in the garden. But when we think of this prohibition, we must not overlook its connection to other laws— stated or implied—that were impressed on Adam's heart in Eden. These include creation ordinances having to do with the most basic interests of life in this world.

- *The Procreation Command:* "So God created man in His own image; in the image of God He created him; male and female He created them. Then God blessed them, and God said to them, 'Be fruitful and multiply; fill the earth and subdue it; have dominion over the fish of the sea, over the birds of the air, and over every living thing that moves on the earth'" (Gen. 1:27-28).

- *The Sabbath Command:* "And on the seventh day God ended His work which He had done, and He rested on the seventh day from all His work which He had done. Then God blessed the seventh day and sanctified it, because in it He rested from all His work which God had created and made" (Gen. 2:2-3).
- *The Work Command:* "Then the LORD God took the man and put him in the garden of Eden to tend and keep it" (Gen. 2:15).
- *The Marriage Command:* "Therefore a man shall leave his father and his mother and be joined to his wife; and they shall become one flesh" (Gen. 2:24).

God did not leave these duties to human subjectivity. Even in the state of sinless integrity when there was no depravity to pervert the desires or blind the vision, God gave Adam objective directions. How much more are objective directions necessary in the state of sin—in which the understanding is blinded, passions are depraved, the conscience is defiled, and the will is perverted!

It is important to grasp the concept that God is our Creator, who made us in His moral image. This connection between the law written on each person's heart and the probationary test confronting Adam is very important. It is important to emphasize the fact that it was written on Adam's heart from the beginning. Thus we have one standard of righteousness from Creation to the final consummation.

Summary of Chapter Two

The inscription of the law on Adam's heart is summarized well by Robert Shaw (*An Exposition of the Confession of Faith,* 192-94).

God having formed man an intelligent creature, and a subject of moral government, he gave him a law for the rule of his conduct. This law was founded in the infinitely righteous nature of God, and the moral relations necessarily subsisting between him and man. It was originally written on the heart of man, as he was endowed with such a perfect knowledge of his Maker's will as was sufficient to inform him concerning the whole extent of his duty, in the circumstances in which he was placed, and was also furnished with power and ability to yield all that obedience which was required of him. This is included in the moral image of God, after which man was created.—Gen. i.27. The law, as thus inscribed on the heart of the first man, is often referred to as *the law of creation*, because it was the will of the sovereign Creator, revealed to the reasonable creature, by impressing it upon his mind and heart at his creation. It is also called *the moral law*, because it was a revelation of the will of God, as his moral governor, and was the standard and rule of man's moral actions. Adam was originally placed under this law in its natural form, as merely directing and obliging him to perfect obedience. . . .

. . . Upon the fall of man, the law, considered as a covenant of works, was disannulled and set aside; but, considered as moral, it continued to be a perfect rule of righteousness. That fair copy of the law which had been inscribed on the heart of the first man in his creation, was, by the fall, greatly defaced, although not totally obliterated. Some faint impressions of it still remain on the minds of all reasonable creatures. Its general principles, such as, that God is to be worshipped, that parents ought to be honoured, that we should do to others what we would reasonably wish that they should do to us—such general principles as these are still, in some degree, engraven on the minds of all men.—Rom. ii. 14, 15. But the original edition of the law being greatly obliterated, God was graciously pleased to give a new and complete copy of it. He delivered it to the Israelites from Mount Sinai, with awful solemnity. In this promulgation of the law, he summed it up in ten commandments; and therefore, it is commonly called the Law of the Ten Commandments. These commandments were written by the finger of God himself on two tables of stone.—Exod. xxxii. 15, 16, xxxiv. 1. The first four commandments contain our duty to God, and the other six our duty to man; and they are summed up by our Saviour in the two great commandments, of loving God with all our hearts, and our neighbour as ourselves.—Matt. xxii. 37-40.

The law written on Adam's heart, substantially the same law written by the finger of God on the two tables of stone at Mount Sinai, is the same standard of righteousness as God writes on every renewed man at conversion.

" 'For this is the covenant that I will make with the house of Israel: After those days,' says the LORD, 'I will put My laws in their mind and write them on their hearts; and I will be their God, and they shall be My people'" (Heb. 8:10). "This is the covenant that I will make with them after those days, says the LORD: I will put My laws into their hearts, and in their minds I will write them" (Heb. 10:16).

CHAPTER THREE

The Law Before Sinai

"Where there is no law there is no
transgression." (Rom. 4:15)

IN THE PREVIOUS CHAPTER, we considered the law written on the hearts of our first parents at creation. Although, as the heads of the human family, they were created perfect and good, they sinned against their Creator and thus lost their proper heritage of life and blessing. This, however, did not negate their responsibility to keep God's perfect rule of righteousness.

After the Fall, all the precepts that had been written on Adam's heart budded forth as God gave His servant Moses, and through him the Israelites, the Ten Commandments. This same law was summarized by our Lord in two great precepts of love to God and love to man. It was exactly this law in its fullness and perfection that was impressed upon the hearts of our first parents and continues to have a place in the hearts of their posterity.

We have seen that the moral law addressed to Adam is also addressed to all creatures. All those created in God's image are obliged to live up to His ethical image. In a later chapter, we will see that at the time of regeneration, the same moral principles are written on the believer's heart resulting in cheerful, loving obedience. That relationship of heartfelt submission to and communion with God is summarized by the author of He-

17

brews: "I will put My laws in their mind and write them on their hearts; and I will be their God, and they shall be My people" (Heb. 8:10).

The Moral Law from Adam to Sinai

We could say that the moral law written on Adam's heart was Adam's lease when God made him the tenant of Eden. But what happened after Adam fell into sin and was evicted from the garden? What role did the moral law play between the Fall and Sinai?

Paul makes clear in Romans 4:15 that where there is no law there is no sin. He adds in Romans 5:13 that "sin is not imputed when there is no law." That raises the question, Could people be held responsible for violating the moral law before the Ten Commandments were revealed?

In this chapter I wish to demonstrate clearly that the violation of each of the Ten Commandments was either severely punished or openly rebuked before Sinai. Before the law was given to Moses, there was indeed sin in the world. We could paraphrase Romans 5:13 this way: "Sin is not recorded against the sinner, when there is no law forbidding it." But if people were punished or rebuked for sin before Sinai, that implies that laws must have been in place, because "where there is no law there is no sin."

The sins punished and rebuked were sins against the perfect law written on Adam's heart at creation. That fact teaches us that the moral law did not have its historical beginning at Sinai. It came to more vivid expression there in the Ten Commandments. And just as the moral law predates the giving of the tablets to Moses on Sinai, so too the moral requirements of the Ten Commandments did not end at Calvary. They remain the standard of obedience today.

Something unique and wonderful happened at Calvary when Christ made atonement for sin. Jesus both paid for sin and upheld the law. He fulfilled the moral law not by bringing an end to it or by setting a new standard of righteousness.

Christians are delivered from sin, not from what is holy, just, and good (Rom. 7:12). They are freed from their disobedience to the commandments, not from the commandments themselves. The believer is not redeemed from what is right; his relationship to what is right has changed. In particular, what has changed is his power and desire to do right, not his duty to do right.

Be careful, then, how you think. False premises produce false conclusions, even when one's reasoning is logically sound. If you assume that the moral law had a beginning at Sinai, you might as well assume that the law had an end at Calvary. But we know that all sinned before Sinai, therefore breaking some commandment—some law—as Romans 4:15 and 5:13 indicate. Before the commandments were given in plain, written form "on tables of stone," the moral law must have been known in some other form. Otherwise the sins of lawbreakers could not have been punished.

Punishable Sins Before Sinai

The First, Second, and Third Commandments
Before the Ten Commandments were revealed on Mount Sinai, the first three commandments (Ex. 20:3-7) were broken by Pharaoh and his people:

- They had false gods—a breach of the first commandment.
- They had false worship—a breach of the second commandment.
- They blasphemed the one true God—a breach of the third commandment.

Therefore, God severely punished the Egyptians with plagues (see Ex. 5-7).

Earlier, Jacob was declared guilty of breaking the second commandment when he failed to "put away the foreign gods that are among you" (Gen. 35:2).

Many other examples of breaking the first, second, and third commandments before Sinai could be cited, but these are sufficient to prove that God held people accountable for these commandments before they were given to Moses.

The Fourth Commandment
When the Israelites broke the Sabbath commandment (Ex. 20:8–11) before Sinai, they were chastised, as the following incident illustrates:

> Now it happened that some of the people went out on the seventh day to gather [bread from heaven], but they found none. And the LORD said to Moses, "How long do you refuse to keep My commandments and My laws? See! For the LORD has given you the Sabbath; therefore He gives you on the sixth day bread for two days. Let every man remain in his place; let no man go out of his place on the seventh day." (Ex. 16:27-29)

The Fifth Commandment
Noah's son Ham broke the commandment to honor one's parents (Ex. 20:12) when he looked on his father's nakedness. As a result, Ham's descendants, the Canaanites, were cursed (Gen. 9:18-29).

Ishmael dishonored his father, Abraham, by mocking him, and he was punished by being cast out (Gen. 21:9–10). Lot's sons-in-law were punished in Sodom for not honoring their father-in-law (Gen. 19:14–15).

The Sixth Commandment
Cain broke the sixth commandment (Ex. 20:13) when he murdered his brother, Abel. As a result, Cain received a punishment greater than he thought he could bear (Gen. 4:13). After the Flood, God declared to Noah the punishment for breaking the sixth commandment: "Whoever sheds man's blood, by man his blood shall be shed" (Gen. 9:6).

In 2 Peter 2:5 we are told that Noah was a preacher of righteousness. Therefore, he must have had a true standard of right-eousness to preach. The one true, perfect standard of right-eousness is the Ten Commandments. Peter's reference to Noah shows us that between Adam and Sinai God made known His commandments by His prophets and preachers.

The Seventh Commandment

The seventh commandment, against adultery (Gen. 20:14), was broken at Sodom, and the Sodomites were punished by their utter destruction (Gen. 19:24-25). The New Testament comments on this incident in Jude 7: "Sodom and Gomorrah, and the cities around them in a similar manner to these, having given themselves over to sexual immorality and gone after strange flesh, are set forth as an example, suffering the vengeance of eternal fire."

In another example, the fellow townsmen of Hamor and his son Shechem were slain by the sword for Shechem's violation of Dinah, Jacob's daughter (Gen. 34:1–26).

The Eighth Commandment

The eighth commandment (Ex. 20:15), which prohibits stealing, was broken when Adam and Eve took of the forbidden fruit. By breaking this commandment, they brought the curse of death upon themselves and their posterity (Gen. 2:16–17).

In Genesis 31 we have the record of Rachel's stealing her father's idols (Gen. 31:19-32), an offense that Jacob considered worthy of death. (He did not know that his own wife Rachel was the culprit.) Jacob's attitude toward stealing in general grew out of a knowledge that it was unlawful in the sight of God. "Where there is no law there is no sin."

The Ninth Commandment

Cain broke the ninth commandment (Ex. 20:16) when he lied to God about his brother's death. "Then the LORD said to Cain, 'Where is Abel your brother?' And he said, 'I do not know. Am I my brother's keeper?'" (Gen 4:9). As a result, the ground was cursed so that his labors would not bring forth fruit from the earth: "When you till the ground, it shall no longer yield its strength to you. A fugitive and a vagabond you shall be on the earth" (Gen. 4:12). How severe is the punishment for breaking the sixth and the ninth commandments!

The Tenth Commandment

When Abimelech coveted Abraham's wife, thus breaking the tenth commandment (Ex. 20:17), he was threatened with death unless he returned her to Abraham (Gen. 20:3). For this sin the Lord closed the wombs of Abimelech's house (Gen. 20:18).

I HAVE OFFERED only a few examples of sins against the Ten Commandments from the time between Adam and Sinai. These examples demonstrate clearly that all the commandments were broken before the Ten Commandments were written on Mount Sinai, and that those guilty of breaking these commandments were either severely punished or sharply rebuked. This point alone should forever put to silence the argument that the commandments had a historical beginning with Moses at Sinai.

Why am I taking a whole chapter to prove that the moral law did not come into being at Sinai?

- To show that the moral law is *for all time.* All have sinned *before* Sinai and *after* Sinai, *before* Calvary and *after* Calvary. Where there is no law there is no sin.
- To demonstrate that the moral law is *for all people.* It is the mandate of the Creator to every person created in His image. When someone becomes a new creature in Christ, he or she does not cease to be a creature under God's authority. A person's basic moral duties do not change.

The Importance of the Law for All

This moral law encoded in the Ten Commandments is of absolute importance and indispensable to all men for at least four reasons.

First, the moral law reveals the holy nature and will of the Creator. The nature of God determines what is right, and the will of God imposes that right standard on humanity as a moral obligation and duty, thus binding every creature to walk accordingly.

Second, the moral law of God convinces creatures of their inability to obey this perfect standard of morality, thus revealing to them not only the sinfulness of their lives, but the sinfulness of their hearts and nature.

Third, when the Spirit brings home to the heart the spirituality of the law (Rom. 7:14), it humbles sinners, giving them a true sense of their sin, and misery apart from Christ.

Fourth, all of this is to lead them to the only remedy for their lost and helpless condition. That remedy is the perfect person and perfect work of Christ the Lord—His perfectly obedient life, His manifestation of the law through His shed blood on the cross, and His provision of an honorable pardon to all who come to God through Him.

This external moral standard of righteousness is of special use to Christians because, although we Christians are not under the condemnation of the law in respect to our justification and acceptance with God, we are still creatures responsible to our Creator. We should not bring our conscience under the curse of the law. But as creatures and as loving children of God, we must bring our whole life, mind, affections, conscience, and will under the law as to our duty to both God and man.

The moral law, therefore, is of special use to the Christian. It shows us how much we are bound to Christ because He has fulfilled its righteous demands and endured the curse in our place, thus making us more thankful to Him for such love and mercy. It also gives us the proper rule for obedience, thus delivering us from all false standards of righteousness.

IN SUMMARY, because God created us in His moral image, we are obliged to keep our Creator's rule of righteousness. This moral code was written on Adam's heart and that of his posterity. Since violation of each commandment resulted in rebuke or punishment before the law was written at Sinai, and since the Bible says where there is no law, no transgression is imputed, we must conclude that these commandments were impressed on the human heart and were a duty before, as well as after, Sinai. This should convince us of the timeless character of God's moral law and make us all the more thankful for Christ's love and mercy.

CHAPTER FOUR

The Giving of the Law at Sinai

"The law is holy, and the commandment holy and just and good." (Rom. 7:12)

THE GREAT CREATOR and possessor of heaven and earth has an indisputable authority to make laws for governing His creatures and to require their obedience. God has opened to us His mind and instructed us in His will. He has made His laws a matter of record. First, He wrote them on the hearts of our original parents. Then He proclaimed them by word of mouth through prophets and preachers, from Adam to Sinai. Later, at Sinai, God inscribed them on tables of stone.

The orthodox Christian church has always referred to the Ten Commandments as the moral law. All the creeds and confessions use the same terminology. It is the moral law as spoken of in Romans 7:12 that will now occupy our attention.

Good Exposing Evil

The apostle is treating the usefulness of the moral law for discovering the sinfulness of sin: "I would not have known sin," he says, "except through the law" (v. 7). The law must first lay down a rule before one can know what sin is—the transgression of that rule. Paul explains, "For I would not have known covetousness," and that the very first inclination of the heart to-

ward evil is sin, "unless the law had said, 'You shall not covet' "
(v. 7)—the tenth commandment. It is evident that Paul is speaking of the moral law, which in its perfect purity exposes the evil
cravings of the heart and, by restraining them, highlights their
sinfulness, thereby provoking greater rebellion. "But sin, taking opportunity by the commandment, produced in me all
manner of evil desire. For apart from the law sin was dead" (v.
8). Although sin is in us, it is not perceived until it is held before the holy, spiritual law of God (v. 14). Then it begins to stir
and rage.

   Before he knew the law, Paul considered himself alive: "I was
alive once without the law" (v. 9). His conscience never troubled him, nor did he apprehend the deadly nature of sin. "But
when the commandment came," that is, when he began to understand the commandment in its spiritual nature, and it pen-
etrated his conscience with divine power, then "sin revived
and I died." He found himself dead in trespasses and sins. "The
commandment, which was to bring life, I found to bring death.
For sin, taking occasion by the commandment," not through
any fault in the commandment, but entirely through his own
fault, "deceived me, and by it killed me (vv. 10–11). What shall
we say then? Are the law and the commandment sin? God forbid. The "law is holy"; all the fault is in us, who abuse the law.
"The commandment [is] holy and just and good" (v. 12).

Moses and Christ

In the very first words of the law, the prologue to the Ten Commandments, the great Creator asserts His own divinity: "I am
the LORD [Jehovah] your God" (Ex. 20:2). He is to be understood
as the whole, undivided Trinity, whose three persons are of
equal majesty, worthy to be acknowledged and worshiped as
deity. That means that the revelation of the Mosaic law came
from the Son of God no less than from the Father and His Spirit.
The law of Moses is the law of Christ.

   Neither John Calvin nor Francis Turretin nor any other respected theologians, creeds, or confessions ever set up an an-

tithesis between Christ and Moses, the law and the gospel, law and grace. The antinomians, however, envision a conflict between each of these pairs, along with a sharp antithesis between the Old and New Testaments. Certainly there are great differences between the old covenant and the new, but a true understanding of them appreciates their proper connection. The fuller we recognize their relationship, the closer we are to grasping biblical Christianity.

The following quotations by Calvin (gathered in J. Graham Miller, *Calvin's Wisdom* [Edinburgh, Scotland: Banner of Truth, 1992]) underscore that relationship:

THE LAW OF GOD

Paul, by the word *law*, frequently intends the rule of a righteous life in which God requires of us what we owe to him, affording us no hope of life, unless we fulfil every part of it, and, on the contrary, annexing a curse if we are guilty of the smallest transgression. *Inst. II:ix.4.*

It is not unusual in Scripture, to seek a description of a pious and holy life, from the Second Table of the Law. *Gen. I:482.*

No mortal will be found who can perform the Law. But in the gospel God receives, with fatherly indulgence, what is not absolutely perfect. *Four Last Books of Moses I:414.*

Free affection is the foundation and beginning of duly obeying the Law, for what is drawn forth by constraint, or servile fear, cannot please God. *Four Last Books of Moses I:381.*

[On Isa. 45:19] The principal end and use of the Law, to invite men to God. *Isa. III:421.*

The peculiar office of the Law [is] to summon consciences to the judgment-seat of God. *John II:140.*

Law and Gospel

[On Heb. 10:1] Under the Law was shadowed forth only in rude and imperfect lines what is under the Gospel set forth in living colours and graphically distinct. . . . To both the same Christ is exhibited, the same righteousness, sanctification, and salvation; and the difference only is in the manner of painting or setting them forth. *Heb. 222.*

When Christ or the Apostles are treating of a perfect life, they always refer believers to the Law. *Four Last Books of Moses III:69.*

He who is the foundation of the covenant of grace, held also the highest rank in the giving of the Law. *Gal. 102.*

The *law* was the grammar of theology, which, after carrying its scholars a short way, handed them over to *faith. Gal. 108.*

If the Law be separated from Christ, it is a dead letter; Christ alone gives it life. *Ezek. II:176, 177.*

In all the ceremonies of the Law [faith] beholds the salvation which has been manifested in Christ. *John II:241.*

Moses had no other intention than to invite all men to go straight to Christ. *John I:217.*

Preaching the Law

We ought to imitate the Prophets, who conveyed the doctrine of the Law in such a manner as to draw from it advices, reproofs, threatenings, and consolations, which they applied to the present condition of the people. *Isa. I:xxx.*

So you can see that John Calvin did not believe there was an antithesis between the law and the gospel but rather taught their vital relationship.

Whatever Happened to Sin?

In place of historic Christianity's emphasis on unity and the antinomian's false antithesis between the law and the gospel, today there is a lack of concern for the moral law. We noted in chapter 1 that this has come about with the secularization of society and the destruction of ethical standards. The fruit of our educational system's attempt to create an amoral society is that, in the home, the school, or the workplace, people do whatever they please.

The church is also partly to blame for this moral decline. Modern theology has "liberated" itself from the absolutes of the Ten Commandments. Many theologians have even done away with Jesus Christ as a historical person. They preach a universal salvation in which the law and the gospel as historically understood are irrelevant.

Equally serious, some evangelical churches have emphasized the love and grace of God while never showing sinners the holiness of the God against whom they have sinned. Scores of people who have been told they are forever saved have never learned of the law of God. Having never understood that sin is separation from God, they have never come to embrace Christ's death on the cross as satisfaction of God's just and eternal wrath against *their* sin. They have failed to grasp the meaning of free, unmerited grace.

In the next chapter we will be considering just how important the connection between law and gospel really is. As a prelude to that chapter, I wish to appeal to one of the most respected theologians in church history.

Ursinus on the Knowledge of Sin and Savior

Almost 450 years ago, Zacharias Ursinus was commissioned by the elector Frederick of Heidelberg to write a catechism for systematic study of the doctrines presented in the Bible. He divided the Heidelberg Catechism into 129 questions in fifty-two lessons. The third question of the catechism is, "Whence knowest thou thy misery?" The answer comes, "Out of the law of God."

Dr. Ursinus in his catechism shows, first of all, man's sinfulness from the law of God and then goes on to set forth how God sent His only begotten Son to be our Savior by meeting the demands of that law. Later in the catechism, Ursinus comes back to show that when Christ has met the demands of the law for us, we stand in a new relationship to the law. The law has become our standard by which we purpose to live in obedience before the God who has saved us.

In the introduction to his commentary on the Heidelberg Catechism, Dr. Ursinus discusses the doctrine of the church and asks, "What are the parts of the Doctrine of the Church, and in what do they differ from each other?" His answer, quoted in part below, shows the true relationship of the law and the gospel, which is so neglected today.

The doctrine of the church consists of two parts: the Law, and the Gospel; in which we have comprehended the sum and substance of the sacred Scriptures. The law is called the Decalogue and the gospel is the doctrine concerning Christ the mediator, and the free remission of sins, through faith. This division of the doctrine of the church is established by these plain and forcible arguments.

1. The whole doctrine comprised in the sacred writings, is either concerning the nature of God, his will, his works, or sin, which is the proper work of men and devils. But all these subjects are fully set forth and taught, either in the law, or in the gospel, or in both. Therefore, the law and gospel are the chief and general divisions of the holy scriptures, and comprise the entire doctrine comprehended therein.

2. Christ himself makes this division of the doctrine which he will have preached in his name, when he says, "Thus it is written, and thus it behoved Christ to suffer, and to rise from the dead the third day; and that repentance and remission of sins should be preached in his name." (Luke 24. 46, 47.) But this em-

braces the entire substance of the law and gospel.

3. The writings of the prophets and apostles, comprise the Old and New Testament, or covenant between God and man. It is, therefore, necessary that the principal parts of the covenant should be contained and explained in these writings, and that they should declare what God promises and grants unto us, viz: his favor, remission of sins, righteousness, and eternal life; and also what he, in return, requires from us: which is faith and obedience. These, now, are the things which are taught in the law and gospel.

4. Christ is the substance and ground of the entire Scriptures. But the doctrine contained in the law and gospel is necessary to lead us to a knowledge of Christ and his benefits: for the law is our schoolmaster, to bring us to Christ, constraining us to fly to him, and showing us what that righteousness is, which he has wrought out, and now offers unto us. But the gospel, professedly, treats of the person, office, and benefits of Christ. Therefore we have, in the law and gospel, the whole of the Scriptures, comprehending the doctrine revealed from heaven for our salvation. (*The Commentary of Dr. Zacharias Ursinus on the Heidelberg Catechism*, trans. G. W. Williard [Phillipsburg, N.J.: Presbyterian and Reformed, n.d.], 2-3)

Thus, it can be seen that in the giving of the law at Sinai, Christ reaffirmed what had already been established with Adam and further pointed the way for man to see his sinfulness and need of a Savior. The gospel, then, related directly to the law by showing Christ's perfect fulfillment of it in our place and promises mercy to those who love its perfect righteousness. Christ's giving the Ten Commandments, reaffirming them in His teaching, and fulfilling them in His ethical behavior show a unity—not an antithesis—between the law and the gospel.

In our next chapter we will consider the importance of that unity between the moral law and the gospel.

CHAPTER FIVE

The Importance of the Moral Law

*"The commandment is a lamp, and
the law is light." (Prov. 6:23)*

IT IS IMPOSSIBLE TO OVERESTIMATE the importance of the moral law.

- Sin is the transgression of the law; therefore, no law, no sin.
- Justification is the verdict of the law; therefore, no law, no need for justification.
- Sanctification is the believer's fulfillment of the law; therefore, no law, no need for sanctification.

The moral law comes into its own and finds its essential fulfillment in the grace manifested in Christ. John Newton was correct when he said,

> Clearly to understand the distinction, connection, and harmony between the Law and the Gospel, and their mutual subserviency to illustrate and establish each other, is a singular privilege, and a happy means of preserving the soul from being entangled by errors on the right hand or the left! Some in the Apostle's time "desired to be teachers of the law; understanding neither

what they said, nor whereof they affirmed." This seems to imply the importance, in a Christian teacher, of a clear understanding of the law in all its connections. And indeed the momentous matter of a sinner's acceptance with God cannot be accurately stated without a distinct view of the subject. (*The Christian Ministry* [London: Banner of Truth, 1958], 1:229)

John Bunyan was also correct when he said, "The man who does not know the nature of the law cannot know the nature of sin. And he who does not know the nature of sin cannot know the nature of the Saviour."

David Calhoun, in his history of Princeton Seminary, observes that on October 3, 1844, Dr. Archibald Alexander (the first professor chosen for Princeton Theological Seminary) preached at the installation of his son James Waddel to the pastorate of the Duane Street Church in New York City. Taking his theme from 2 Timothy 2:15—"Rightly Dividing the Word of Truth"—Dr. Alexander presented many insights discovered during his own long ministry.

Alexander described the preacher as a workman. "Two sorts of men should . . . be excluded from the gospel ministry: first, those who will not work; secondly, those who know not how to perform their work aright." The wise preacher, Alexander continued, must know how to rightly divide the word of truth. Among other things, that means that he arrange and present biblical truth in such a manner "that it may be most easily and effectually understood." He will "declare the whole counsel of God," but "in due order, at proper times, and with a wise reference to the strength and spiritual attainments of our hearers."

Most importantly for Alexander,

"a good workman will so divide the word of truth, as clearly to distinguish between the law and the gospel; between the covenant of works and the covenant of grace." By insisting on this point, the Princeton professor said, Luther began the Reformation; he called it "the article of the standing or falling of the Church." If the preacher misses the mark here, "you will find him bewildered, and bewildering his hearers everywhere else." He will preach "another gospel" which "brings no good news to lost sinners; but sets men at work to get into paradise at the old gate, which was long ago shut up, and has for thousands of years been guarded by the fiery-flaming sword of Divine justice." While preaching grace, Dr. Alexander said, the good workman will not neglect to set forth "the holy law of God in its spirituality, extent, and binding obligation . . . for where there are none sick, there will be no need of a physician; and where no law is preached, there will be no conviction of sin, and none crying out, 'what must we do to be saved?'" "Let the law be faithfully proclaimed, as binding on every creature, and as cursing every impenitent sinner," stated the preacher, "and let the utter inability of man to satisfy its demands be clearly set forth, not as an excuse, but as a fault; and then let the riches of grace in Christ Jesus be fully exhibited and freely offered, and let all—however great their guilt—be urged to accept of unmerited pardon, and complete salvation." (David B. Calhoun, *Princeton Seminary*, Volume 1, *Faith and Learning 1812–1868* [Edinburgh: Banner of Truth, 1994], 274-76)

Six Reasons Why the Law and Gospel Are Essential

1. The Message of the Whole Bible

The first reason for the importance of this subject is that *the whole Bible is either law or gospel*, that is, the law and the gospel are the principal parts of divine revelation. They are so vitally connected and related to each other, that an accurate knowledge of either cannot be obtained without the other. As noted earlier, they are the center, the sum, and the substance of all the parts of divine truth.

- The history of the Old and New Testaments narrates the acts of men and women done either in conformity or in opposition to the moral law, either in belief or in unbelief of the gospel.
- All the warnings of the Old and New Testaments are threatenings of the law or the gospel. For example, John 3:18 says, "He who believes in Him is not condemned; but he who does not believe is condemned already." Yes, there are gospel threatenings. Another example is 2 Thessalonians 1:7-9: ". . . and to give you who are troubled rest with us when the Lord Jesus is revealed from heaven with His mighty angels, in flaming fire taking vengeance on those who do not know God, and on those who do not obey the gospel of our Lord Jesus Christ. These shall be punished with everlasting destruction from the presence of the Lord and from the glory of His power."
- Every prophecy of Scripture is a declaration of things obscure and future connected with either law or gospel, or both.
- Every promise is related to either the law or the gospel, or both.
- Every admonition, reproof, or exhortation is with reference to the law or the gospel, or both.

How important, then, it is to exercise our best efforts to distinguish between the two! It is certain that the closer we get to a clear view of (1) the difference between the law and the gospel, (2) the connection between them, and (3) how they serve to establish each other, the more we will understand the Holy Scriptures and the will and mind of God, and the more useful we will be in His service.

2. Central Truths

The second reason for the importance of this subject is that *the law is one of three great truths of the Bible* that stand or fall together. These truths are:

- The law of God.
- The cross of Christ.
- The righteous judgment of almighty God.

These three are vitally connected. If we do away with the law, there is no sin, and therefore no need of a Savior. If we do away with the cross, we have no answer to the sin problem. If there is no righteous judgment of almighty God, there is no point to talking about sin or a Savior.

In some respects the most wonderful description of the work of Christ on the cross in all the Bible is Isaiah 42:21: "The LORD was pleased . . . to make the law great and glorious" (NASB). Where did He do that? On the cross. It is often said of Jesus that He came to fulfill the law, but here it says, He came to "magnify the law and make it honorable" (NKJV). He came to give new luster and glory to the holy law of God so that the world might see and understand that the law is holy and just and good.

When God wrote the law upon Adam's heart in creation, he magnified the law. He showed it to be a great and holy and righteous law. When God spoke the law from Sinai, He magnified the law and made it glorious. But most of all when Christ died on the cross, He gave radiance, greatness, and majesty to the law of God in the sight of all the world. When we look to the cross, one of the things we see is Christ's magnifying God's holy law and making it honorable by giving us an honorable pardon. Not a sentimental pardon, but an *honorable* one.

Jesus magnified the holiness and justice of the law by bearing its curse (see 2 Cor. 3:9–11). He explained the law's meaning, He expressed its character, He embodied its duties, and He endured its penalty.

Our Lord obeyed the law from the cradle to the grave. He delighted to do the will of His Father. "I have come . . . to do Your will, O God" (Heb. 10:7). His delight in obeying the Father showed to all the world that happiness and the chief good of the creature are by-products of keeping God's holy law.

When teaching boys and girls the commandments, I like to ask them what would it be like . . .

(1) if everyone would love and serve God?

(2) if no one would worship idols, money, or pleasure?

(3) if no one would curse or take the Lord's name in vain?

(4) if everyone would see how good God is to have provided one day a week to worship, rest, and do acts of necessity and mercy?

(5) if all children would obey their parents, and everyone would honor those who are in authority, such as teachers and civil authorities; and therefore we would have no need for police, jails, or courts?

(6) if no one would murder, and we could feel safe anywhere at night?

(7) if no one would commit adultery, so that we would have no broken homes?

(8) if no one would steal, and we would have no need for locks or locksmiths?

(9) if no one would bear false witness, that is, lie?

(10) if no one would covet, and all people were content with who they were and what they possessed?

Their answer usually is, "It would be heaven!"

The reason it would be heaven is that we would all be like Christ. He is the most free being in the universe, as well as the most wise. He knows the nature of all things from the beginning to the end. He tasted the joys of heaven. He drank from all eternity the rivers of God's pleasure. Yet, when He stood in our nature, He delighted in the law of God. Yes, God's law was within His heart. One evidence of that was that Jesus was subject to His parents. In one sentence, Luke 2:51 summarizes twelve years of His life: "He went down with them and came to Nazareth, and was subject to them." Thus, He honored God's law, not as a legalist or a Pharisee; nor was He an antinomian. He magnified the law and made it honorable by His obedience.

Evangelism

The third reason showing the importance of this subject is that *the law is important to evangelism*—an issue dear to the heart of every true preacher and every true Christian. The following church fathers certainly thought so:

Luther: "The law must be laid upon those that are justified, that they may be shut up in the prison thereof, until the righteousness of faith comes—that, when they are cast down and humbled by the law, they should fly to Christ. The Lord humbles them, not to their destruction, but to their salvation. For God wounds, that he may heal again. He kills, that he may quicken again" (*God's Law and God's Children* [Cape Coral, Fl.: Grace Baptist Church, 1988], 70).

Augustine: "The conscience is not to be healed if it is not wounded. Thou preachest and pressest the law, the judgment to come, with much earnestness and importunity. He which hears, if he is not terrified, if he is not troubled, is not to be comforted" (Ibid., 70).

Tyndale: "It becomes the preacher of Christ's glad tidings, first through the opening of the law, to prove all things sin, that proceed not of the Spirit, and of faith in Christ; and thereby to bring him unto the knowledge of himself, and of his misery and wretchedness, that he might derive help."

Writing to John Firth: "Expound the law truly, to condemn all flesh, and prove all men sinners, and all deeds under the law (before mercy has taken away the condemnation thereof) to be sin, and damnable, and then as a faithful minister, set abroad the mercy of our Lord Jesus Christ, and let the wounded conscience drink of the water of life. And thus shall your preaching be with power, and not as hypocrites. And the Spirit of God shall work with you; and all consciences shall bear record unto you that it is so" (Ibid., 64).

Archbishop Usher: "What order is there used in the delivery of the word, for the begetting of faith?"

Answer: "First, the covenant of the law is urged, to make sin, and the punishment thereof, known; whereupon the sting of conscience pricks the heart with a sense of God's wrath, and makes a man utterly to despair of any ability in himself to obtain everlasting life. After this preparation the promises of God are propounded; whereupon the sinner, conceiving a hope of pardon, looks to God for mercy" (Ibid., 62).

Charles Haddon Spurgeon: "The divine Spirit wounds before he heals, he kills before he makes alive. We usually draw a distinction between law-work and gospel-work; but law-work is the work of the Spirit of God, is so far a true gospel-work that it is a frequent preliminary to the joy and peace of the gospel. The law is the needle which draws after it the silken thread of blessing, and you cannot get the thread into the stuff without the needle: men do not receive the liberty wherewith Christ makes them free till, first of all, they have felt bondage within their own spirit driving them to cry for liberty to the great Emancipator, the Lord Jesus Christ. This sense or spirit of bondage works for our salvation by leading us to cry for mercy" (Ibid., 60-61).

In the immortal volume *Pilgrim's Progress,* John Bunyan, in his inimitable way, gives us a vivid picture of the law and evangelism in the Interpreter's House:

Then I took him by the hand, and led him into a very large parlour that was full of dust, because never swept; the which after he had reviewed a little while, the *Interpreter* called for a man to sweep. Now when he began to sweep, the dust began so abundantly to fly about, that *Christian* had almost therewith been choked. Then said the *Interpreter* to a *Damsel* that stood by, bring hither Water and sprinkle the room; the which when she had done, it was swept and cleansed with pleasure.

Chr. Then said *Christian,* What means this?

Inter. The *Interpreter* answered, This *parlour* is the heart of a man that was never sanctified by the sweet Grace of the Gospel: The *dust* is his Original Sin, and inward Corruptions that have defiled the whole man. He that began to sweep at first, is the *Law;* but she that brought Water, and did sprinkle it, is the *Gospel.* Now, whereas thou sawest that so soon as the first began to sweep, the dust did so fly about, that the room by him could not be cleansed, but that thou was almost choked therewith; this is to show thee, that the Law, instead of cleansing the heart (by its working) from Sin, doth revive, put strength into, and increase it in the soul, even as it doth discover and forbid it, for it doth not give Power to subdue.

Again, as thou sawest the *Damsel* sprinkle the room with Water, upon which it was cleansed with pleasure; this is to shew thee, that when the Gospel comes in, the sweet and precious influences thereof to the heart, then, I say, even as thou sawest the *Damsel* lay the dust by sprinkling the floor with Water, so is Sin vanquished and subdued, and the soul made clean, through the Faith of it, and consequently fit for the King of Glory to inhabit. (*Pilgrim's Progress* [Edinburgh: Banner of Truth, 1979], 26-27)

In days gone by, children learned the commandments before they learned John 3:16, because only then did John 3:16 have real meaning and purpose.

John Elliot's first translation to the Indians was not John 3:16 but the Ten Commandments. His first sermon likewise dealt with the commandments. Did John Elliot think the Indians would be saved by the Ten Commandments? Of course not, but the commandments would show them why they needed to be saved: They were lawbreakers, and they needed a law-keeper to be their substitute.

John Paton, a great Presbyterian missionary to the New Hebrides, first taught the cannibals the commandments. Why? Men will never be properly interested in a relationship with the Redeemer until they see the terrible breach in the relationship between the Creator and the creature. The Commandments are the Creator's moral mandate for His creatures. The sharp needle of the law makes way for the scarlet thread of the gospel. The law is indispensable in biblical, God-centered evangelism.

Knowledge Necessary for Salvation

The fourth evidence of its importance is that *the law reveals the two knowledges necessary for salvation.* John Calvin begins his *Institutes of the Christian Religion* by describing these two knowledges necessary for salvation—the knowledge of God and that of ourselves. The two are interconnected and are revealed in the law.

> *1. Without knowledge of self there is no knowledge of God*
> Nearly all the wisdom we possess, that is to say, true and sound wisdom, consists of two parts: the knowledge of God and of ourselves. But, while joined by many bonds, which one precedes and brings forth the other is not easy to discern. In the first place, no one can look upon himself without immediately turning his thoughts to the contemplation of God, in whom he "lives and moves" (Acts 17:28). For, quite clearly, the mighty gifts with which we are endowed are hardly from ourselves; indeed, our very being is nothing but subsistence in the one God. Then, by these benefits shed like dew from heaven upon us, we are led as by rivulets to the spring itself. Indeed, our very poverty better discloses the infinitude of benefits reposing in God. The miserable ruin, into which the rebellion of the first man cast us, especially compels us to look upward. Thus, not only will we, in fasting and hungering, seek thence what we lack; but, in being aroused by fear, we shall learn humility. For, as a veritable world of miseries is to be found in mankind, and we are thereby despoiled of divine rai-

ment, our shameful nakedness exposes a teeming horde of infamies. Each of us must, then, be so stung by the consciousness of his own unhappiness as to attain at least some knowledge of God. Thus, from the feeling of our own ignorance, vanity, poverty, infirmity, and—what is more—depravity and corruption, we recognize that the true light of wisdom, sound virtue, full abundance of every good, and purity of righteousness rest in the Lord alone. To this extent we are prompted by our own ills to contemplate the good things of God; and we cannot seriously aspire to him before we begin to become displeased with ourselves. For what man in all the world would not gladly remain as he is—what man does not remain as he is—so long as he does not know himself, that is, while content with his own gifts, and whether ignorant or unmindful of his own misery? Accordingly, the knowledge of ourselves not only arouses us to seek God, but also, as it were, leads us by the hand to find him.

2. *Without knowledge of God there is no knowledge of self*

Again, it is certain that man never achieves a clear knowledge of himself unless he has first looked upon God's face, and then descends from contemplating him to scrutinize himself. For we always seem to ourselves righteous and upright and wise and holy—this pride is innate in all of us—unless by clear proofs, we stand convinced of our own unrighteousness, foulness, folly, and impurity. Moreover, we are not thus convinced if we look merely to ourselves and not also to the Lord, who is the sole standard by which this judgment must be measured. For, because all of us are inclined by nature to hypocrisy, a kind of empty image of righteousness in place of righteousness itself abundantly satisfies us. And because nothing appears within or around us that has not been contaminated by great immorality, what is a little less vile pleases us as a thing most pure—

so long as we confine our minds within the limits of human corruption. Just so, an eye to which nothing is shown but black objects judges something dirty white or even rather darkly mottled to be whiteness itself. Indeed, we can discern still more clearly from the bodily senses how much we are deluded in estimating the powers of the soul. For if in broad daylight we either look down upon the ground or survey whatever meets our view round about, we seem to ourselves endowed with the strongest and keenest sight; yet when we look up to the sun and gaze straight at it, that power of sight which was particularly strong on earth is at once blunted and confused by a great brilliance, and thus we are compelled to admit that our keenness in looking upon things earthly is sheer dullness when it comes to the sun. So it happens in estimating our spiritual goods. As long as we do not look beyond the earth, being quite content with our own righteousness, wisdom, and virtue, we flatter ourselves most sweetly, and fancy ourselves all but demigods. Suppose we but once begin to raise our thoughts to God, and to ponder his nature, and how completely perfect are his righteousness, wisdom, and power—the straightedge to which we must be shaped. Then, what masquerading earlier as righteousness was pleasing in us will soon grow filthy in its consummate wickedness. What wonderfully impressed us under the name of wisdom will stink in its very foolishness. What wore the face of power will prove itself the most miserable weakness. That is, what in us seems perfection itself corresponds ill to the purity of God. (ed. John T. McNeill, trans. Ford Lewis Battles [Philadelphia: Westminster Press, 1960], 2:35-38)

The law reveals the character of God. His law comes from His nature. The nature of God determines what is right, and then the will of God imposes that standard upon all His creatures as a moral obligation. Because His will flows from His nature, if the law is perfect (Ps. 19:7), we can expect that His nature is no less perfect.

Christ was perfect. How do we know? He kept the law perfectly. He was the law personified. Christ manifested the Father by conforming to the Father's holy will. "For in Him dwells all the fullness of the Godhead bodily" (Col. 2:9).

The law reveals the condition of man. To walk up to someone and say, "All have sinned" does not bring conviction—unless the person knows what sin is. "Sin is the transgression of the law" (1 John 3:4 KJV). "By the law is the knowledge of sin" (Rom. 3:20). And that is what brings conviction. Man is not answerable to an abstract law, but to God. Behind the law is the Lawgiver. Therefore, to find fault with the law is to find fault with the Lawgiver. The law is not the arbitrary edicts of a capricious despot but the wise, holy, loving decrees of One who is jealous for His own glory and for the good of His people.

The Way of Holiness

The fifth reason for the importance of this subject is that *the law provides a real standard for direction in the way of holiness.*

What special use is there of the moral law to Christians? Although Christians are delivered from the law as a way of justification, so that they are not justified or condemned by it, yet it does inform them of their duty as those who have been justified and are growing along the road of sanctification. As the only perfect standard of righteousness, the law tells us the right way to travel, though it gives no strength for the journey.

In Ephesians 6, Paul appeals to the fifth commandment when he instructs children, "Honor your father and mother . . . that it may be well with you and you may live long on the earth" (vv. 2-3). The first reason Paul gives for children to obey their parents in the Lord is that "this is right." The law alone tells us what is right. And while a Christian is under grace, that grace never changes what is right. The commandments are right, holy, just, and good.

Let me emphasize that grace never changes what is right. It does change our relationship to what is right by giving us a desire and the power to do right, but it *never* redefines the standard of right and wrong.

The Spiritual Life

The sixth reason for the importance of this topic is that *the law and gospel are inseparable in the spiritual life.* Submission to the law of the Lord is not reserved for a "second work of grace." Those who genuinely trust Jesus as Savior also understand that they are called out of sin and into a life of obedience. There is no place for the complacency of so-called "carnal" Christians and no place for the pride of so-called "spiritual" or "higher-life" Christians.

Paul says in Romans 8:1–4,

> There is therefore now no condemnation to those who are in Christ Jesus, who do not walk according to the flesh, but according to the Spirit. For the law of the Spirit of life in Christ Jesus has made me free from the law of sin and death. For what the law could not do in that it was weak through the flesh, God did by sending His own Son in the likeness of sinful flesh, on account of sin: He condemned sin in the flesh, that the righteous requirement of the law might be fulfilled in us who do not walk according to the flesh but according to the Spirit.

Notice that "those who are in Christ . . . do not walk according to the flesh but according to the Spirit" (vv. 1, 4). In other words, they have a growing desire to obey the law of the Lord. They do so out of a deep gratitude for His fulfilling the law for them and His enduring the curse in their place.

IF YOU ARE UNCONVERTED and you have picked up this book, you may be wondering, *Of what use is the moral law to me?* The moral law has something to say to all creatures, and you are one of God's creatures. The Ten Commandments are the Creator's mandates to you.

1. The law shows you the holy nature and will of God, your duty, binding you to walk accordingly.
2. The law shows you the sinful pollution of your nature, heart, and life.
3. The law will humble you in the realization of your sin and misery, and awaken your conscience to flee from the wrath to come. My unconverted friend, these are the commandments of your almighty Judge—the Judge of all the earth. In His court you are guilty.
4. The law reveals your need of Christ.
5. The law is a schoolmaster to lead you to Christ for mercy and forgiveness.
6. If you continue in your present way of sin and disobedience, the law will leave you without excuse, and you will continue to be under the curse of the law of God. "Cursed is everyone who does not continue in all things which are written in the book of the law, to do them" (Gal. 3:10).

These truths should convince any reasonable person of the importance of the moral law in the work of the gospel.

CHAPTER SIX

Difficulties (1): The Meanings of *Law*

*"The law is good if one uses it
lawfully." (1 Tim. 1:8)*

ONE OF THE DIFFICULTIES in dealing with the subject of the law
is the word itself. It is used in many different ways in the Bible.
Sometimes *law* refers to the whole Bible; sometimes it refers to
the Pentateuch (the first five books of the Bible); sometimes it
refers to the ceremonial system; other times it refers to the civil
or judicial code, which was peculiar to Israel as a theocracy. The
different meanings of the word in expressions such as "the law
of Moses," "the law of Christ," "the law of sin," and "the law of
love," make it very difficult to exegete specific texts accurately.

Samuel Bolton, a renowned seventeenth-century scholar, was
so highly esteemed by his peers that he was chosen as one of the
Westminster divines, who met in 1643 to introduce a second Reformation in English Christianity. He was a successful minister
of parishes in London and later became the vice-chancellor of
Cambridge University. In a little volume entitled *True Bounds of
Christian Freedom*, ([reprint; Edinburgh: Banner of Truth, 1977],
54-56), Bolton addresses the antinomian controversy of his day.
He says this about the scriptural uses of the word *law*:

(1) What is meant by the word "law"? I answer: the
word which is frequently used for "the law" in the Old

47

Testament is "Torah." This is derived from another word which signifies "to throw darts," and comes to signify "to teach, to instruct, to admonish"; hence it is used for any doctrine or instruction which teaches, informs, or directs us: as, for example, in Proverbs 13:14: "The law of the wise is a fountain of life, to depart from the snares of death." Here "law" is taken in a large sense for any doctrine or direction which proceeds from the wise; so, too, in Proverbs 3:1 and 4:2.

In the New Testament the word "law" is derived from another word which signifies "to distribute," because the law distributes, or renders to God and man their dues.

In brief, this word "law," in its natural signification both in the Old and New Testaments, signifies any doctrine, instruction, law, ordinance, or statute, divine or human, which teaches, directs, commands, or binds men to any duty which they owe to God or man. So much, then, for the first matter.

(2) In what senses is this word "law" used in Scripture? I shall not trouble the reader with all the uses of the word, but shall confine myself to the chief of them:

(i) It is sometimes taken for the Scriptures of the Old Testament, the books of Moses, the Psalms, and the Prophets. So the Jews understood it in John 12:34: "We have heard out of the law that Christ abideth for ever." So also in John 15:25: "This cometh to pass, that the word might be fulfilled that is written in their law. They hated me without a cause" (Ps. 35:19). Similarly, we have 1 Cor. 14:21: "In the law it is written," where the apostle is repeating the words of Isa. 28:11, and he says they are written in the law.

(ii) The term "law" is sometimes used as meaning the whole Word of God, its promises and precepts, as in Ps. 19:7: "The law of the Lord is perfect, converting the soul." Conversion is the fruit of the promise. Neither justification nor sanctification is the fruit of the law alone. The law commands but gives no grace, so that here the psalmist includes the promise of grace in his use of "law"; or else conversion, as he speaks of it here, does not mean regeneration.

(iii) "Law" is sometimes taken for the five books of Moses, as in Gal. 3:21: "If there had been a law given which could have given life, verily righteousness should have been by the law." Likewise, in John 1:45: "We have found him of whom Moses in the law . . . did write." Similarly in Luke 24:44: "All things must be fulfilled which were written in the law of Moses," meaning the five books of Moses; see also Gal. 4:21.

(iv) "Law" is used for the pedagogy of Moses, as in John 5:46: "Had ye believed Moses, ye would have believed me: for he wrote of me." See also Josh. 1:7-8.

(v) Sometimes "law" is used for the moral law alone, the Decalogue, as in Rom. 7:7, 14, and 21.

(vi) . . . Sometimes "law" refers to the ceremonial law, as in Luke 16:16.

(vii) Sometimes "law" refers to all the laws, moral, ceremonial, and judicial, as in John 1:17: "The law was given by Moses, but grace and truth came by Jesus Christ": "grace" in opposition to the moral law, "truth" in opposition to the ceremonial law which was but a shadow. Thus Chrysostom comments on this passage: "The ceremonial law was given right up to the time of the coming of the seed promised to Abraham."

Among all these different usages, the controversy lies in the last mentioned, where the word "law" signifies the moral, judicial, and ceremonial law. In respect of two of these varieties of law, we find considerable agreement; the main difficulty concerns the moral law.

Moral, Ceremonial, and Civil

Since there are so many uses of the term *law,* in any serious study of the law it is absolutely necessary to make a proper distinction between the moral, ceremonial, and civil laws. Failure to make clear and proper distinctions will always lead to either legalism or antinomianism.

All of the time-tested, respected historic creeds, confessions, and catechisms, as well as Calvin's *Institutes of the Christian Religion,* divide the laws given to Israel at Sinai into ceremonial, civil, and moral.

Although the Bible does not use these three words to divide the law, we discover these distinct uses of the term *law* as we bring all the Scriptures to bear on the subject. We are not like the Jehovah Witnesses, who deny the Trinity because they do not find the word *Trinity* in the Bible. We believe in a triune God because the Scriptures clearly show us the work and attributes of all three persons of the Trinity. They are all active in Creation, redemption, and providence.

By bringing the whole Bible to bear on the subject of the laws given at Sinai, we learn that some laws pertained to procedures in worship and not to ethical conduct. Other laws stipulated the civil duties of Israel as a theocratic nation and were not binding on the Gentile nations. Still others were the Creator's moral mandates for the conduct of all His creatures. These moral laws are eternal and unchangeable.

Dr. Zacharias Ursinus clarifies the three kinds of laws and their differences.

> WHAT ARE THE PARTS OF THE LAW, AND WHAT THEIR DIFFERENCES? . . .
>
> The divine law is ordinarily divided, or considered as consisting of three parts; the moral, the ceremonial and the judicial.
>
> The *moral law* is a doctrine harmonising with the eternal and unchangeable wisdom and justice of God, distinguishing right from wrong, known by nature, engraven upon the hearts of creatures endowed with reason in their creation, and afterwards often repeated and declared by the voice of God through his servants, the prophets; teaching what God is and what he re-

quires, binding all intelligent creatures to perfect obedience and conformity to the law, internal and external, promising favor of God and eternal life to all those who render perfect obedience, and at the same time denouncing the wrath of God and everlasting punishment upon all those who do not render this obedience, unless remission of sins and reconciliation with God be secured for the sake of Christ the mediator.

Harmonising with the eternal and unchangeable wisdom of God: That the law is *eternal* is evident from this, that it remains one and the same from the beginning to the end of the world. We were also created, and have been redeemed by Christ and regenerated by the Holy Spirit, that we might keep this law, or love God and our neighbor as it requires, both in this and in the life to come. "I write no new commandment unto you, but an old commandment which you had from the beginning" (1 John 2:7).

Afterwards often repeated: God repeated the law of nature which was engraven upon the mind of man: 1. Because it was obscured and weakened by the fall. 2. That what was still left in the mind of man might not be regarded as a mere opinion or notion, and so at length be lost.

Ceremonial laws were those which God gave through Moses in reference to ceremonies, or the external solemn ordinances which were to be observed in the public worship of God, with a proper attention to the circumstances which had been prescribed; binding the Jewish nation to the coming of the Messiah, and at the same time distinguishing them from all other nations; and that they might also be signs, symbols, types and shadows of spiritual things to be fulfilled in the New Testament by Christ. *Ceremonies* are external solemn actions which are often to be repeated in the same manner and with the same circumstance, and which have been instituted by God, or by men to be observed in the external worship of God, for the sake of order, propriety and

signification. The ceremonies which have been instituted by God, constitute divine worship absolutely;
while those which have been instituted by men, if they
are good, merely contribute to divine worship.

The judicial laws were those which had respect to the
civil order or government, and the maintenance of external propriety among the Jewish people according to
both tables of the Decalogue; or it may be said that they
had respect to the order and duties of magistrates, the
courts of justice, contracts, punishments, fixing the limits of kingdoms, &c. These laws God delivered through
Moses for the establishment and preservation of the
Jewish commonwealth, binding all the posterity of
Abraham, and distinguishing them from the rest of
mankind until the coming of the Messiah; and that they
might also serve as a bond for the preservation and government of the Mosaic polity, until the manifestation of
the Son of God in the flesh, that they might be certain
marks by which the nation which was bound by them,
might be distinguished from all other nations, and
might at the same time be the means of preserving
proper discipline and order, that so they might be types
of the order which should be established in the kingdom
of Christ. (*The Commentary of Dr. Zacharias Ursinus on the
Heidelberg Catechism*, trans. G. W. Williard [Phillipsburg,
N.J.: Presbyterian and Reformed, n.d.], 490-91)

It is important to note that in the precepts of the moral law
we find the goal of all other laws. The ceremonial law would
not have been necessary, nor would it make sense, if it were not
for sins against the moral law. The civil laws applied the principles of the moral law to the specific context of national Israel.
Though we are not bound to the particular civil laws themselves, they embody ideals that remain valid to us, though in
new ways.

The division of the law into moral, ceremonial, and civil is
clear to us with a New Testament in our hands and Christ's hav-

ing come. But was there any way for Old Testament believers to recognize these distinctions? Yes, there are good reasons to believe that some Old Testament saints did see a difference.

1. Consider the drastic difference in how God revealed them. He revealed the ceremonial and civil laws to Moses, who wrote them on vellum or parchment. But God Himself wrote the Ten Commandments, and not on perishable skins, but on tables of stone (Deut. 9:10)—a symbol of the permanence of the Ten Commandments.

2. Some statements of Old Testament believers indicate a conscious distinction between the moral, civil, and ceremonial laws. For example, David contrasts them when he says, "You do not desire sacrifice . . . You do not delight in burnt offering" (Ps. 51:16). Here David is speaking about religious ceremonies. Yet God *does* desire conformity to the moral laws "You shall not commit adultery" and "You shall not murder," which David disobeyed. That violation made it necessary for him to offer sacrifices—provided he did so with a broken and contrite heart. When offered in true faith, such sacrifices appealed to and prefigured the one and only real and final sacrifice, Jesus Christ.

Likewise, in Psalm 40:6-8, David contrasts the ceremonial law with the law written on his heart: "Sacrifice and offering You did not desire; my ears You have opened; burnt offering and sin offering You did not require. Then I said, 'Behold, I come; in the scroll of the Book it is written of me. I delight to do Your will, O my God, and Your law is within my heart."

Surely these statements do not mean that David felt no obligation to observe the external ceremonial ordinances. They were the means by which Christ was administered to him through shadows and types. But these words indicate that David saw a difference between ceremonial and moral legislation. His words anticipated the end of the one and the continuance of the other. Likewise, Jeremiah, the prophet, saw the difference (Jer. 7:22-23), as did Samuel (1 Sam. 15:22).

3. The ceremonial law also evidenced its temporary nature by its inability to make perfect those who observe it: "For the law, having a shadow of the good things to come, and not the

very image of the things, can never with these sacrifices, which they offered continually year by year, make those who approach perfect" (Heb. 10:1). "And every priest stands ministering daily and offering repeatedly the same sacrifices, which can never take away sins" (Heb. 10:11). The Holy Spirit testified of something better—the one oblation of Jesus (Heb. 10:14-17; cf. Jer. 31:33ff).

4. Another indication that the Old Testament saints saw the difference is that the predictions of the coming sufferings of Christ were given in ceremonial terms (Isa. 53:11; Dan. 9:25-27; Zeph. 1:7-8). These show the temporary character of the ceremonial law. It was abrogated at Calvary when the real sacrifice was offered once and for all.

In any consideration of the law of God, these distinctions must be very clear. Where they are not, there will always be confusion and error—in some cases, heresy.

It is of the utmost importance, therefore, to discern the differences between the ceremonial law, which pertained to the worship of Israel and prefigured Christ; the civil or judicial laws, which detailed the duties to Israel as a nation (having their roots in the moral law, particularly in the second table); and the moral law, by which the Creator governs the moral conduct of *all* creatures for *all* times.

A Summary of the Differences

1. The moral laws were spiritual and had to do with internals and externals. That is implied by the tenth commandment, which speaks of the desires of the heart that lead to outward violation of the other commands: "You shall not covet your neighbor's house; you shall not covet your neighbor's wife, nor his manservant, nor his maidservant, nor his ox, nor his donkey, nor anything that is your neighbor's" (Ex. 20:17). This commandment suggests that the other commandments are to be interpreted in terms of internal, spiritual issues, as well as outward actions. Paul makes the same point in Romans 7:14, when he says, "We know that the law is spiritual." He attributes his own

conversion to this very fact: "What shall we say then? Is the law sin? Certainly not! On the contrary, I would not have known sin, except through the law. For I would not have known covetousness unless the law had said, 'You shall not covet'" (v. 7).

It was this fact that drove him from a legalistic, Pharisaic view of the commandments to an evangelical view and led him to say, "Therefore the law is holy, and the commandment holy and just and good" (v. 12). If Romans 7 teaches us anything, it teaches that the law is spiritual and requires internal as well as external obedience.

2. The ceremonial and civil laws were types and figures. The moral law is neither type nor figure. What was a sin in Eden is a sin now and until the end. Before Sinai, it was a sin to take the Lord's name in vain, to steal, to commit adultery, to murder, to lie, to covet, etc., and it will be a sin to do so as long as there is a Holy God in heaven and there are people on earth. As B. H. Carroll has said, "The time will never come when it will be right for a man to kill, to steal, to commit adultery, to covet, and no matter who does any of these things, whether saint or sinner, it is sin."

3. The prophets foretold the end of the ceremonial and civil laws, but not the end of the righteous standard of the moral law.

4. Christ and His apostles, in different places and at different times in the New Testament, declared the end of the ceremonial and civil laws, but never an end of the righteous standard of the moral law (cf. Heb. 7:11-20; 8:8-13; 9:1-4).

5. When the purposes of the other laws ended, the laws themselves ended, but the purpose of the Ten Commandments will never end. It will always be necessary

- to inform everyone of the holy nature and will of God.
- to inform all people of their duty to God and their neighbor, and to bind them to walk accordingly.
- to convince sinners of their inability to keep the law, and drive them to Christ.
- to humble sinners by showing them the sinful pollution of their natures, hearts, and lives, and thus help them

gain a clear sight of their need of Christ and the perfection of His obedience.

- to show true believers how much they are bound to Christ for His fulfilling the law for them and thus make them more thankful to Him for all He has done for them.

- to give true believers an objective standard of righteousness, thus directing them to the right road to travel (though it gives no strength for the journey).

The moral law, as a rule, can no more be abolished or changed than the nature of good and evil can be abolished or changed. The substance of the law is the sum of doctrine concerning piety toward God, charity toward our neighbors, and temperance and sobriety toward ourselves. For believers, the moral law is abrogated in respect to its power to justify; but it remains full of force to direct us in our lives. It condemns sin in the faithful, though it cannot condemn the faithful for sin. It is not the way of life, but it is the rule of life.

While distinctions between moral, ceremonial, and judicial laws are of the utmost importance, a caution is necessary. It would be wrong to imagine that any of God's statutes given to Moses were arbitrary or that the three kinds of law were unrelated. Both ceremonial and judicial statutes of the Old Testament were firmly anchored in the moral law. For this reason a special reverence was given to the pure moral law—the Ten Commandments. The whole of the Mosaic system was built upon the "ten words."

Were it not for offenses against the righteousness of God (the moral law), there would have been no need for a Savior and His great salvation. A Messiah and His cross rise out of a broken moral law, a law that must be satisfied if anyone is to be saved. The ceremonial law therefore depicts the person, offices, and acts of Christ, which everywhere call attention to moral principles. The ceremonies point forward to Christ as the answer to a broken moral law.

Civil laws administered moral and ceremonial regulations on

a nationwide scale. Each judicial statute built its pedagogy for young believers around a moral core. Thus, even ceremonial and civil laws in Israel rose ultimately from the righteousness of God.

All three kinds of law are woven tightly into a unified covenant administration in Moses. Seldom can a text be labeled entirely moral, ceremonial, or civil. It would be a mistake to read through Exodus or Deuteronomy and attempt to label one verse ceremonial and another moral. In many instances all three are intertwined so that it is impossible to make such neat iden-tifications.

The Ten Commandments are the glaring exception. This fea-ture of Moses' law has tempted some to declare all statutes moral. It has led others to declare all ordinances null and void for the Christian. Both conclusions constitute a cavalier ap-proach to the interpretation of the Bible. The one would shackle Christians under a new bondage. The other would rob the Christian of a large segment of Scripture.

IN THIS CHAPTER we have examined one of the difficulties in dealing with the subject of the law, that is, the different ways the little word *law* is used in the Bible. In our next chapter we will consider some further areas of difficulty—antinomianism, legalism, and Christian liberty.

CHAPTER SEVEN

Difficulties (2): Law, Liberty, and Antinomianism

*"If the Son makes you free, you shall
be free indeed." (John 8:36)*

ANOTHER DIFFICULTY THAT ARISES in any serious study of the law is the topic of Christian liberty in contrast to both antinomianism and legalism. There is a razor-sharp line between antinomianism and legalism or between Christian liberty and antinomianism. As Christ was crucified between two thieves, likewise the law is often crucified between legalism and antinomianism.

It is important that the rights of the law be vindicated and that the liberties of grace be maintained. The object of this chapter is twofold: (1) to uphold the law so that it does not threaten Christian liberty, and (2) to establish grace so that the law is not made void and believers are not exempted from their duties to God and man.

Christian Liberty Not Lawlessness

Salvation in Christ is liberation, and the Christian life is one of liberty. Christ has set us free (Gal. 5:1; cf. John 8:32, 36). His liberating work is not basically social, political, or economic improvement, as is sometimes suggested. It is liberation from the law as a means to salvation and liberation from the power of sin and superstition.

First, *Christians have been set free from the law as a system of salvation.* Being justified by faith in Christ, they are no longer under God's law but under His grace (Rom. 3:19; 6:14–15; Gal. 3:23-25). Their standing with God (the "peace" and "access" of Rom. 5:1–2) is assured because they have been accepted and adopted in Christ. It does not ever depend on what they do, nor will it ever be imperiled by what they fail to do. They live, not by being perfect, but by being forgiven.

Second, *Christians have been set free from sin's dominion* (John 8:34-36; Rom. 6:14-23). They have been supernaturally regenerated and made alive to God through union with Christ in His death and risen life (Rom. 6:3–11). The desire of their heart now is to serve God in righteousness (Rom. 6:18, 22). Sin's dominion involves not only constant acts of disobedience but also a constant disregard for God's moral law, rising sometimes to resentment or even hatred toward the law. Now, however, being changed in heart, motivated by thankfulness for the gift of grace, and energized by the Holy Spirit, Christians "serve in the newness of the Spirit and not in the oldness of the letter" (Rom. 7:6).

Third, *Christians have been set free from superstitions,* including the idea that matter and physical pleasure are intrinsically evil. Against this idea, Paul insists that Christians are free to enjoy all created things as God's good gifts (1 Tim. 4:1–5), provided they do not transgress the moral law, or hinder their own spiritual well-being or that of others (1 Cor. 6:12–13; 8:7–13).

Notice in these three aspects of Christian liberty that Christians have *not* been set free from responsibility to obey the moral law. Believers are exhorted in the New Testament to love one another on the express ground that it is a requirement of the moral law. "For you, brethren, have been called to liberty; only do not use liberty as an opportunity for the flesh, but through love serve one another. For all the law is fulfilled in one word, even in this: 'You shall love your neighbor as yourself.' But if you bite and devour one another, beware lest you be consumed by one another!" (Gal. 5:13–15).

If the "liberty" possessed by the Galatians consisted in freedom from the obligation to obey the moral law, it would be
strange that these very precepts should be urged as an authority against their using liberty as an occasion to the flesh. Paul,
whatever some of his professed admirers have been, was assuredly a better reasoner than this would make him. The liberty of the gospel includes an exemption from the precepts of
the ceremonial law, and from the curse or condemning power
of the moral law; and these were privileges of inestimable value.
They were, however, susceptible of abuse. To guard against
this, the holy *precept* of the law, notwithstanding the removal
of its penalty, is held up by the apostle in all its native and in-
alienable authority. To the same purpose, the apostle, writing
to the believing Romans, inculcates brotherly love and purity
from the authority of the moral law.

> Owe no one anything except to love one another, for he
> who loves another has fulfilled the law. For the com-
> mandments, "You shall not commit adultery," "You
> shall not murder," "You shall not steal," "You shall not
> bear false witness," "You shall not covet," and if there
> is any other commandment, are all summed up in this
> saying, namely, "You shall love your neighbor as your-
> self." Love does no harm to a neighbor; therefore love
> is the fulfillment of the law. And do this, knowing the
> time, that now it is high time to awake out of sleep; for
> now is our salvation nearer than when we first believed.
> The night is far spent, the day is at hand. Therefore let
> us cast off the works of darkness, and let us put on the
> armor of light. Let us walk properly, as in the day, not
> in revelry and drunkenness, not in licentiousness and
> lewdness, not in strife and envying. But put on the Lord
> Jesus Christ, and make no provision for the flesh, to ful-
> fill its lusts. (Rom. 13:8–14)

It is hard to imagine how anyone can read this passage without perceiving that the precepts of the moral law are still bind-

ing on believers. Those who fail to acknowledge this truth will have to bear the consequences of their lawlessness.

Some Falsely Labeled Antinomian

The Bible and history prove that not everyone who has been accused of lawlessness is an antinomian. Where the graciousness of free grace is preached in all its fullness, the accusation of antinomianism has always been heard. The Lord Jesus Himself was accused of this. When, in contrast to John the Baptist, He did not live in solitude but rather mingled with others—even with publicans and notorious sinners—it didn't take long for people to say, "Look, a glutton and a winebibber, a friend of tax collectors and sinners!" (Luke 7:34). The Pharisees and rabbis repeatedly accused Him of not honoring the law of Moses but setting it aside instead.

The apostle Paul fared no better. His doctrine of grace was also labeled antinomianism. In Romans 3:8 he tells us how some people twisted his message: "And why not say, 'Let us do evil that good may come'?—as we are slanderously reported and as some affirm that we say." Thus, also Paul was accused of teaching antinomianism.

It is also interesting to note that C. H. Spurgeon was charged with the errors of antinomianism. In a sermon preached on March 16, 1856, he said,

> I am rather fond of being called an Antinomian, for this reason, that the term is generally applied to those who hold truth very firmly and will not let it go. But I should not be fond of being an Antinomian. We are not against the law of God. We believe it is no longer binding on us as the covenant of salvation; but we have nothing to say against the law of God. "The law is holy; we are carnal, sold under sin." None shall charge us truthfully with being Antinomians. We do quarrel with Antinomians; but as for some poor souls who are so inconsistent as to say the law is not binding, and yet try to keep it with all

their might, we do not quarrel with them! They will
never do much mischief. But we think they might learn
to distinguish between the law as a covenant of life and
a direction after we have obtained life. (*The New Park
Street Pulpit* [Grand Rapids: Zondervan, 1963], 2:132)

These examples prove that not everyone accused of being an
antinomian is in fact one. We must not allow such false accu-
sations to blind us to the fact that there is real antinomianism,
and it needs to be addressed as a very dangerous and damning reality today.

The word *antinomianism* dates back to the days of the Reformation, though the doctrine of antinomianism itself is as old as
the gospel. The spirit of antinomianism is to forsake the rule of
God. But the truth is that whatever disowns or weakens the authority of the law overturns the gospel and all true religion. The
law and the gospel are friends. They mutually serve to establish each other. The work of the Spirit is to fulfill the law in us
"that the righteous requirement of the law might be fulfilled in
us" (Rom. 8:4). God and His perfect law are so united that you
cannot be at enmity with one without being at enmity with the
other.

What Exactly Is Antinomianism?

The Encyclopedia of Christianity gives a list of antinomian errors.
This list provides a profile of the antinomian system as it has
taken various forms in the course of history:

1. The law is made void by grace. Justification by faith
   alone renders good works unnecessary.
2. Since good works are unnecessary, obedience to the law
   is not required of justified persons.
3. God sees no sin in the justified, who are no longer
   bound by the law, and is not displeased with them if
   they sin.
4. God therefore does not chastise justified persons for sin.

5. Nor can sin in any way injure the justified.
6. Since no duties or obligations are admitted in the gospel, faith and repentance are not commanded.
7. The Christian need not repent in order to receive pardon of sin.
8. Nor need he mortify sin; Christ has mortified sin for him.
9. Nor ought he be distressed in conscience upon backsliding, but he should hold fast to a full assurance of his salvation in the midst of the vilest sins.
10. Justifying faith is the assurance that one is already justified.
11. The elect are actually justified before they believe, even from all eternity.
12. Therefore they were never children of wrath or under condemnation.
13. Their sin, as to its very being, was imputed to Christ so as not to be theirs, and His holiness is imputed to them as their sanctification.
14. Sanctification is no evidence of justification, for assurance is the fruit of an immediate revelation that one is an elect person.
15. No conviction by the law precedes the sinner's closing with Christ, inasmuch as Christ is freely offered to sinners as sinners.
16. Repentance is produced not by the law, but by the gospel only.
17. The secret counsel of God is the rule of man's conduct.
18. God is the author and approver of sin, for sin is the accomplishment of His will.
19. Unless the Spirit works holiness in the soul, there is no obligation to be holy or to strive toward that end.
20. All externals are useless or indifferent, since the Spirit alone gives life.

Although the above list is incomplete, it is far from being incoherent. Logical sequence is evident throughout. Propositions

1–14 are consequences illegitimately drawn from justification by faith; 15–16, from the free offer and effectual power of the gospel; 17-20, from the sovereignty of God. Antinomianism is to be understood primarily as an abuse of justifying grace in disparaging the authority of the law (1–6), in minimizing the need for repentance (6-9), and even for faith (10–12), by nullifying sanctification (13–14), and exaggerating assurance (9, 10, 14), and by denying the instrumentality of the law in conversion (15–16). Although 17-20 may be regarded as underlying the fallacious reasoning in 1–16, they do not warrant a simple identification of antinomianism with hyper-Calvinism. While accepting the ethical force of Rabbi Duncan's dictum, we might alter it from a logical point of view, and assert that the only or root heresy is Pelagianism. The root error of "free will" in the sense of ability limiting obligation is the counterpart of the main spring of antinomianism in 17, the affinity of which with 11, the logical foundation of evangelical antinomianism, is evident.

During the Reformation. Luther vs. Agricola. Johannes Agricola of Eisleben (1492–1566), one of Luther's most intimate associates in the German Reformation, developed a one-sided view of justification by faith, for which Luther found himself obliged to coin the epithet "antinomian." Agricola and his followers are reported to have taught the following erroneous and dangerous theses:

1. Men are not to be prepared for the gospel or conversion by the preaching of the law.
2. Repentance is not to be taught out of the Decalogue or any law of Moses, but from the violation of the Son of God in the gospel.
3. When thou art in the midst of sin, only believe, and thou art in the midst of salvation.
4. The law is not worthy to be called the Word of God.
5. A believer is above all law and all obedience.
6. Good works profit nothing to salvation. Ill works tend not to damnation.

7. Our faith and New Testament religion were unknown to Moses.

Although he had ignored Agricola's earlier opposition to Melanchton's insistence on preaching the law, Luther protested in 1537 against any identification of the doctrine of justification with antinomianism and elicited a recantation from Agricola. Luther firmly maintained the necessity for preaching the law before as well as after conversion. Against an antinomian tenet curiously akin to Barthian emphases, Luther remarks, "But thus they preposterously put the Cart before the Horse, teaching the Law after the Gospel, and wrath after grace" (Luther's letter to Guttel against the antinomians). Luther taught three uses of the law: (1) to manifest sin; (2) to instruct as a schoolmaster to Christ; (3) "That the Saints might know what works God requires, in which they can exercise obedience towards God" (Luther, *Werke*, 31.1.485). Rutherford devotes nearly 100 pages of his *Spiritual Antichrist* to a demonstration that antinomian errors find no support in Luther, despite some unguarded utterances on his part. (*The Encyclopedia of Christianity* [Wilmington, Del.: National Foundation for Christian Education, 1964], 1:270-78)

Forms of Antinomianism

In the May/June 1995 issue of the *Banner of Sovereign Grace Truth*, Reverend C. Harinck, pastor of the Gereformeerde Gemeente of Houten, the Netherlands, points out three of the most common forms of antinomianism. I will summarize Harinck's exposition of these in the remainder of this chapter.

Theological Antinomianism
We find theological antinomianism particularly with the English theologians, Crisp, Eaton, and Saltmarch. They placed such emphasis upon God's eternal election, justification from eternity, and the immediate assurance of sonship by the Holy Spirit, that they deviated to antinomianism as a logical consequence of their doctrine. If believers have indeed been ordained unto

salvation from eternity, then nothing—not even their sins—can undo this salvation. If believers are justified from eternity and have been acquitted from all their sins, what law could yet accuse them? If God's children have the immediate knowledge that they are the children of God, would they yet need the witness of their good works?

The English antinomians believed that the law has no function, for believers possess all things. Nothing needs to be merited, and therefore nothing needs to be feared. The believer is a partaker of eternal election, eternal justification, and the immediate assurance of his sonship. Where then is the necessity of the law? It only denigrates grace, so they taught, and subjects the redeemed Christian only by renewal to the yoke of bondage.

This form of antinomianism proceeds from the quarters of hyper-Calvinism. A doctrine of election taken to its logical extreme led to an unbiblical view that the believer already possesses everything from eternity. Such a life is too high and too free to be bound to the law. Thus these theologians did not consider the grace of God to imply holy obligations.

When the Lord says to Israel, "I am the LORD your God, who brought you out of the land of Egypt, out of the house of bondage," He did not continue, "and therefore there is no law. You are free men. You have My redemption and are led only by My Spirit." On the contrary, the Lord says, in effect, "I have redeemed you and *therefore,* You shall have no other gods before Me." In other words, "Since I have redeemed you, therefore keep My commandments, do what is pleasing to Me, preserve your redemption, and fight against the Evil One."

The mistake the English antinomians made was that *they separated what God had joined together*. Justification and sanctification cannot be separated.

Exegetical Antinomianism
We encounter another kind of antinomianism among those who make a radical separation between the Old and New Testaments. Among modern preachers and evangelical move-

ments it is commonplace to teach that the law belongs to the Old Testament. Thus there is no longer any room for the law; faith alone matters now. The originator of this view in particular is J. Nelson Darby, the founder of the Plymouth Brethren. He taught that during the period of grace (the New Testament), the law no longer has any significance for believers. He referred to the covenant of works as a fable and considered the law to have been set aside. The only thing required, so he taught, is faith in Christ.

This teaching has engendered the view that our decision for Christ is the only thing that matters. One must permit Jesus to come into his heart, and beyond that one is under no obligation to the law. The only concern for our children is whether they have made a decision for Christ. The law as a mirror for the uncovering of sin and as a rule of life is of no significance. As long as one has made a decision for Jesus, one need not be devoted to a life in harmony with God's law as proof of the uprightness and veracity of his faith. Christianity thus becomes more a matter of decision than a manner of life. Ultimately, this results in a "carnal Christianity" void of true Christian living.

Unmerited grace, however, makes one subject to evangelical obligations. A sanctified life is what manifests the fruits of true faith.

Practical Antinomianism

Practical antinomianism is the most progressive form of antinomianism, that which is not in name only, but in actual deed. It should not be ascribed to all who, on purely dogmatic grounds or on the basis of the difference between the Testaments, maintain that the law no longer has any significance for the Christian. Practical antinomians not only teach upon theological or exegetical grounds that the believer had nothing to do with the law, but they also practice lawlessness. They reason, *Since God accepts me as I am, I need not be very particular when it comes to the law. And since I already have been fully forgiven from eternity, it doesn't really matter how I live.* Yes, they even dare to practice what the apostle Paul condemns: "Shall we continue to sin that grace may abound?" (Rom. 6:1). "We are delivered from the law," so they exclaim, "and therefore we can do as we please. Our sin only makes grace abound all the more."

Such people resemble the man who breaks the speed limit and says, "It does not matter in my case, for I am not under the law. I have been redeemed and set free. I may do as I please. It is only my old man which does wrong things. My new man remains unscathed in the midst of all this." What a dreadful error! What an appalling abuse of the doctrine of God's grace! In response to this view, the apostle pronounces the apostolic anathema, "God forbid" (Rom. 6:2 KJV)!

BECAUSE ANTINOMIANISM is rampant today, the topic of law and liberty remains very relevant. Determining the truth among all the voices in the controversy can be difficult. Some set up the law for justification. Others deny the law as a direction for sanctification. Thank God that there are still others who realize that our freedom is from the curse and the penalty of the law, not from the guidance, direction, and commands of the law.

That is the orthodox view. Our freedom from the penalties of the law is not freedom from its precepts for holy living. In this way, grace and law are both established while true Christian liberty is affirmed.

CHAPTER EIGHT

Principles for Understanding the Ten Commandments

"Give me understanding and I shall keep Your law; indeed, I shall observe it with my whole heart." (Ps. 119:34)

WE HAVE CONSIDERED in an earlier chapter that the moral law was clearly written on Adam's heart at creation. After the Fall, this clear law was defaced, although not totally obliterated. According to Romans 2:14–15, some faint impressions of it still remain on the hearts of reasonable men. As with a wheat field or corn field after harvest, you can still recognize what crop was there.

At Mount Sinai, our Creator graciously gave a new, objective copy of this perfect moral law, the Ten Commandments. They are said to be written by the finger of God (Ex. 32:15–16), which was not true of the ceremonial and civil laws. Some commentators make much of this point. I believe it is important to note that the commandments have no relationship to time or place as did the ceremonial and civil laws. The Ten Commandments are given to all creatures for all times and in all places. They are the summary of the eternal standard of right moral conduct— a fixed, objective standard of righteousness.

Every creature under heaven should be concerned about his or her duty to the almighty Creator and judge of all the earth. Therefore, the question What duty does the Creator require of His creatures? is always relevant. The biblical answer is that God requires personal, perfect, perpetual obedience to His revealed will. The next logical question is Where do we find

God's revealed will regarding moral conduct? The biblical answer is that it is summarized in the Ten Commandments.

Yet the Decalogue must be understood according to the rest of Scripture, not according to merely human judgment or philosophy. We must bring together the explanations found in different portions of Scripture and not confine ourselves to the simple letter of the commandments expressed in such a brief form. The Bible is like a great statute book of God's kingdom, having in it the whole body of heavenly law—the perfect rules for a holy life and a sure promise of grace. Sometimes the Ten Commandments are referred to as the "ten words." They are a short summary of the moral duty for all God's creatures. Though they are brief, the substance contained in them is infinite. The whole of Scripture is a commentary on the Ten Commandments as to moral duty.

Part of that commentary is in the book of Exodus. Before we examine principles for interpretation, a few words about the prologue to the commandments are in order. Exodus 20 begins, "And God spoke all these words, saying, 'I am the LORD your God, who brought you out of the land of Egypt, out of the house of bondage'" (vv. 1–2).

The significance of this prologue cannot be overstated. The Ten Commandments were of God's making, of God's speaking—a law stemming from God's nature. God asserts His own authority to enact this law in general. "I am the LORD" who commands all that follows in Exodus 20:1–17. He proposes Himself as the sole object of the religious worship He requires in the first four commandments.

Two reasons for obedience are implied in this prologue. The first is that *He is the Lord—Jehovah God*. That means that He is:

- Self-existent.
- Eternal.
- Founder of all beings and all powers—the Creator.

As Creator, He has a right to command His subjects.

The second reason for obedience is that He is not only Creator, *He is their God* in a special way—"Your God." *He is their*

Redeemer—He brought them out of Egypt. Since this was a re-demptive act, we see at the outset of the commandments God's redeeming love, grace, and mercy. Thus, we must never sepa-rate God's love, grace, and mercy from His commandments.

With that in mind, we are ready to consider seven principles or rules for a right understanding and use of the Ten Com-mandments.

Principles for Understanding the Commandments

The First Principle

The Decalogue must be understood as all Scripture must be un-derstood: according to the explanation and application that the Prophets, Christ, and the apostles have given it. How did the Prophets, Christ, and the apostles use the commandments? They treated the commandments as authoritative in their teach-ing and preaching (see, for example, 2 Sam. 12:9; Matt. 5; Rom. 13:8–10; 1 Cor. 6:9–11; 1 Tim. 1:9–10).

The Second Principle

The commandments demand both external and internal obe-dience. Addressing the will and the heart, as well as actions, they require more than merely outward conformity. They also require inward affection. The commandments forbid not only evil acts but evil desires and inclinations. They go to the mind—including the will and the affections—thereby calling for obe-dience from the whole man.

How do we know that the commandments demand both ex-ternal and internal obedience? "We know that the law is spiri-tual," Paul wrote in Romans 7:14. And our Lord explained in Matthew 5:21–44 that the commandments pertain to attitudes and desires, as well as actions. For example:

- Not only murder, but hate.
- Not only adultery, but lusting.
- Not only stealing, but coveting.

We know too that the tenth commandment teaches us how the others are to be observed. It forbids a covetous heart. This is the commandment the Pharisees missed. The tenth commandment is also the commandment used in Paul's conversion. He wrote,

> What shall we say then? Is the law sin? Certainly not! On the contrary, I would not have known sin except through the law. For I would not have known covetousness unless the law had said, "You shall not covet." But sin, taking opportunity by the commandment, produced in me all manner of evil desire. For apart from the law sin was dead. I was alive once without the law, but when the commandment came, sin revived and I died. (Rom. 7:7-9)

The tenth commandment deals with the internal. A proper understanding of this rule will keep us from becoming legalists and Pharisees.

The Third Principle

There is a negative and a positive side to the commandments. Where sin is forbidden, a duty is commanded. For example, in the sixth commandment, murder is forbidden; therefore protection of life is commanded. It is the sixth commandment that supports a just war: Soldiers are responsible for protecting the lives of citizens.

The eighth commandment, "You shall not steal," implies the positive mandate to protect the property of others. The seventh commandment, "You shall not commit adultery," has the positive goal of protecting chastity, which can be done in many ways.

So with all the commandments, where a sin is forbidden, a duty is commanded. Each commandment has a positive side and a negative side.

The Fourth Principle

Where a sin is forbidden, the inducement or the occasion of it is also forbidden. Whatever leads to or induces sin becomes sin itself. For example, not only is adultery forbidden but also all that leads to adultery is forbidden. If certain reading material incites sinful lusts, then the reading of that material is a sin against the seventh commandment. Pictures, magazines, television programs, movies—anything that leads to breaking any of the commandments should be avoided.

If you want to be free from a contagious disease, you must avoid contact with places through which or persons through whom the infection is spread. Just as quarantine signs used to mark houses for certain diseases, whatever draws us into sin should be considered off limits.

Proverbs 5:8 says of the adulterous woman, "Remove your way far from her, and do not go near the door of her house." Jesus had this same principle in mind when He said, "If your right eye causes you to sin, pluck it out. . . . And if your right hand causes you to sin, cut it off" (Matt. 5:29–30).

The Fifth Principle

The commandments of the second table of the law (the fifth through the tenth, which have to do with our neighbor) must yield to the commandments of the first table of the law (which have to do directly with God) when there is any conflict between our duties to the first and the second tables of the law. For example, if parents command their children to do something against God, the children should seek to obey God rather than men.

Another aspect of this principle is that the commands of the first table are not to be kept for the sake of the commands of the second table, but rather the commands of the second table are to be kept for the sake of the first table. Worship of God and service to Him are not performed out of respect for man, but our duty toward man is performed out of respect for God. All sin is first and foremost against Him. "Against You, You only, have I sinned, and done this evil in Your sight—that You may be found just when You speak, and be blameless when You judge" (Ps. 51:4; cf. Luke 15:18).

In other words, we do not love and serve God for man's

sake, but we do love man for God's sake. It is also true that God is not truly loved unless our neighbor is loved, and neither is our neighbor truly loved when God is not loved. "If someone says, 'I love God,' and hates his brother, he is a liar; for he who does not love his brother whom he has seen, how can he love God whom he has not seen? (1 John 4:20; cf. Matt. 22:38, 40).

The duties we perform to our neighbor (duties of the second table) should flow from a threefold respect for God.

- Obedience to His authority. He commanded the duties of the second table.
- Conformity to His example. ". . . that you may be sons of your Father in heaven; for He makes His sun rise on the evil and on the good, and sends rain on the just and on the unjust" (Matt. 5:45).
- A proper hope and expectation of His eternal reward. "Love your enemies, do good . . . and your reward will be great" (Luke 6:35). (If God promises this as added incentive, don't despise it. Don't be more pious than the Bible.)

The Sixth Principle
It is essential that we consider the purpose for which each commandment was given, its true meaning and what God intends. When we see this, we will know the commands are in our best interest. "The commandment is holy and just and for our good" (Rom. 7:12 MOFFAT). You need only imagine how much better the world would be if everyone kept the commandments. The law of God is not detrimental to us. It is masterfully designed for our good.

The Seventh Principle
Whatever is forbidden or commanded of us, we are bound, according to our position, to discourage or encourage in others

according to the duty of their positions. For example, an employer should not coerce or allow employees to break a commandment when it is within his authority to keep them from doing so. The same principle applies to other authority relationships, such as that between parents and children.

God's law not only forbids our sinning but also forbids our being accessory to the sins of others when it is within our power to do something about it. An accessory is one who, not being present, contributes to or assists in the commission of an offense. An accessory "after the fact" assists or shelters the evil doer.

There are at least five ways in which we can be accessory to or partakers of the sins of others.

1. *By issuing unrighteous decrees, thereby ordering other people to do unrighteous deeds:* For example, David merely wrote a letter to Joab ordering him to send Uriah to the forefront of battle. But hear the Lord's charge against David through the prophet Nathan: "Why have you despised the commandment of the LORD, to do evil in His sight? *You have killed Uriah* the Hittite with the sword" (2 Sam. 12:9).

We are guilty of breaking a commandment if we are accessory to the breaking of that commandment. Ordering the cause of sin is sin.

2. *By not hindering others from sin when it is within our power, ability, or sphere of authority:* Eli was guilty for not hindering his sons' vile behavior. "He did not restrain them" (1 Sam. 3:13). Allowing one's children to break the commandments under the guise of love is sin. The mark of a loving father is that he chastens his sons (Heb. 12:6-7). His love has as its aim the glory of God. "For this is the love of God, that we keep His commandments. And His commandments are not burdensome" (1 John 5:3).

3. *By counseling or provoking others to sin:* Paul wrote, "Fathers, do not provoke your children to wrath" (Eph. 6:4). To provoke someone to anger is to promote a murderous spirit (Matt. 5:21-22).

4. *By consenting to another's sin:* Although Saul of Tarsus did

not cast one stone at Stephen, "Saul was consenting to his death" (Acts 8:1).

5. *By setting a bad example.*

A Summary of Principles for Understanding and Using the Commandments

1. The commandments must be understood according to the explanation that the Prophets, Christ, and the Apostles gave them.
2. The commandments are spiritual, and therefore they go to the heart, requiring internal obedience and inward affection, not merely outward conformity. They forbid not only the acts of sin but also the desire and inclination to sin.
3. There are both positive and negative sides to the commandments. Where sin is forbidden, a duty is commanded.
4. Where sin is forbidden, the inducements or the occasion that leads to the sin is forbidden. We are to stay away from temptation as one stays away from a contagious disease.
5. The commandments that deal with our relationships with other people must yield to the commandments that deal with our relationship to God. If there is a conflict between the duties of the first and second tables, the first comes first.
6. It is essential to consider the end (that is the purpose and design) of the commandments.
7. Whatever is forbidden or commanded of us, we are bound, according to our position, to discourage or encourage in others according to the duty of their positions.

To these seven principles we may briefly add two more:

8. What is forbidden is at no time to be done, but what is required is to be done only when the Lord affords opportunity.

9. The beginning and the end, as well as the sum, of all the commandments is love. "Love is the fulfilling of the law" (Rom. 13:10).

These principles give us a proper understanding for the right use of the commandments and will spare us from legalism, pharisaism, and antinomianism.

CHAPTER NINE

Does Human Inability Make God Unjust?

"The law is holy, and the commandment holy and just and good." (Rom. 7:12)

THE QUESTION IS OFTEN ASKED, Is God unjust to require from man what he has no ability to perform?

Before David Brainard, the great missionary to the American Indians, was converted, four things caused him to be angry with God. One of the things that greatly disturbed him was the strictness of the divine law.

> For I found it was impossible for me, after my utmost pains, to answer its demands. I often made new resolutions, and as often broke them. I imputed the whole to carelessness and the want of being more watchful, and used to call myself a fool for my negligence. But when, upon a stronger resolution, and greater endeavors, and close application to fasting and prayer, I found all attempts fail; then I quarreled with the law of God, as unreasonably rigid. I thought if it extended only to my outward actions and behaviors, I could bear with it; but I found it condemned me for my evil thoughts and sins of my years, which I could not possibly prevent.
>
> I was extremely loathe to own my utter helplessness in this matter; but after repeated disappointments,

78

thought that, rather than perish, I could do a little more still; especially if such and such circumstances might but attend my endeavors and strivings. I hoped that I should strive more earnestly than ever if the matter came to extremity—though I never could find the time to do my utmost, in the matter I intended—and this hope of future, more favorable circumstances, and of doing something great hereafter, kept me from utter despair in myself and from seeing myself fallen into the hands of a sovereign God, and dependent on nothing but free and boundless grace. (*The Life and Diary of David Brainard*, ed. Jonathan Edwards [Chicago: Moody Press], 64-65)

David Brainard was not alone in his attitude toward God's holy, just, and good law. Many have felt that God is unjust in demanding obedience to a law that no natural man can perform. One objection that always surfaces when the Ten Commandments are taken seriously is, Since no one has the ability to keep them, why take any of them seriously?

The Fourfold State of Man

In order to answer questions about God's justness, we must have some understanding of the biblical teaching on the fourfold state of man. Thomas Boston, in his wonderful book *Human Nature in Its Fourfold State* (London: Banner of Truth, 1964) divides this fourfold state as follows:

1. The State of Innocence.
2. The State of Nature.
3. The State of Grace.
4. The State of Glory or the Eternal State.

Let me give a brief overview of these four different states of man.

The State of Innocence

In the state of innocence Adam had:

- Perfect rectitude of mind, that is, uprightness in principles, freedom from error, and accuracy in judgment.
- Perfect sanctity of will.
- Perfection of power.

He had a copy of God's law written on his heart. As a key is fitted to all the wards of a lock and can open it, so Adam had power suited to all of God's commandments and could obey them perfectly. Therefore, before we charge God with being unjust and requiring what was impossible, we must consider how man was created. "Truly, this only I have found: that God made man upright, but they have sought out many schemes" (Eccl. 7:29).

If I believed that God made man the way he is and then condemned him for being that way, I would curse God and die. Such a God would be a monster!

God does command and require what unregenerate sinners cannot perform. But Adam, as he was created, was able to perform personal, perfect obedience. God's standards do not change. He still commands personal, perfect obedience to all His commandments.

To the question, Is not God unjust to require what men do not have the ability to perform? I answer:

- Yes, God is unjust, *unless* He first gave the ability to perform what He requires.
- Yes, God is unjust, *unless* man, by his own will, brought this inability upon himself.
- Yes, God is unjust in requiring that which man cannot perform, *unless* such a requirement is designed to lead him to acknowledge and deplore his inability.

The real problem with those who commiserate with man in his present plight is that they fail to ask how he got into this condition. They rashly charge God with being unjust even though He created man good, innocent, and free not to sin.

When you see sickness, death, war, pain, murder, rape, robbery, and lawlessness, you must ask, How did this come about? The answer is *sin—man's sin!* How did the prodigal son reach the point where he longed to eat the feed of pigs? By living in sin! Just as the prodigal's sin plunged his life into poverty and despair, the sin of Adam plunged the entire human race into a fallen state marked by hardship, strife, and futility.

The State of Nature

Man in his fallen state has a corrupted nature and is in need of renewal by the Holy Spirit. This is where you are if you are not converted. There are two uses of the law in this state.

1. It curbs evil in the world, as well as in the church.
2. It brings a knowledge of sin. The law accuses, convinces, and condemns all those who are not regenerated, because they are unrighteous before God and subject to His righteous judgment.

> Now we know that whatever the law says, it says to those who are under the law, that every mouth may be stopped, and all the world may become guilty before God. Therefore by the deeds of the law no flesh will be justified in His sight; for by the law is the knowledge of sin. (Rom. 3:19-20)

> I would not have known sin except through the law. For I would not have known covetousness unless the law had said, "You shall not covet." (Rom. 7:7)

Thomas Boston in his book *Human Nature in Its Fourfold State* called this:

- The sinfulness of man's natural state: "The LORD saw that the wickedness of man was great in the earth, and

that every intent of the thoughts of his heart was only
evil continually" (Gen. 6:5).
- The misery of man's natural state: "We . . . were by nature children of wrath, just as the others" (Eph. 2:3).
- Man's utter inability to recover himself: "For when we
were still without strength, in due time Christ died for
the ungodly" (Rom. 5:6).

In the state of nature, a person has no ability to do anything
spiritually good. "No one can come to Me unless the Father
who sent Me draws him" (John 6:44).

The State of Grace

When a person is restored to spiritual life in Christ, he or she
is in the state of grace. There are many uses of the law in respect
to those who have been regenerated by the Holy Spirit. Having been made alive and empowered by the indwelling Spirit
of God, they are enabled to obey God's commands.

In this life, that obedience is far from complete, and believers must always fall back upon the saving work of Christ on the
cross. But because God's children have been delivered from
both the penalty and the power of sin, growth in genuine obedience is possible and is to be sought with all one's heart.

The Eternal State—The State of Glory

In the fourth state of man, human nature is perfectly restored
and glorified. This will be the state of God's children after this
life. Even then the law will have its use, for although the preaching of it and the whole ministry of the church shall have ceased,
there will still remain in the elect a knowledge of the law, as perfect obedience to all its demands and full conformity with God
will be wrought in them. The law will, therefore, accomplish the
same purpose in the life to come—when we shall be fully transformed into the image of God—as it did in our nature before
the Fall.

There are six aspects of this eternal state.

1. *Death.* "For I know that You will bring me to death, and to the house appointed for all living" (Job 30:23).
2. *The difference between the righteous and the wicked in their death.* "The wicked is driven away in his wickedness: but the righteous hath hope in his death" (Prov. 14:32 KJV).
3. *The resurrection.* "Do not marvel at this; for the hour is coming in which all who are in the graves will hear His voice and come forth—those who have done good, to the resurrection of life, and those who have done evil, to the resurrection of condemnation" (John 5:28–29).
4. *The general judgment.*

> When the Son of Man comes in His glory, and all the holy angels with Him, then He will sit on the throne of His glory. All the nations will be gathered before Him, and He will separate them one from another, as a shepherd divides his sheep from the goats. And He will set the sheep on His right hand, but the goats on the left. Then the King will say to those on His right hand, "Come, you blessed. . . ." Then He will also say to those on the left hand, "Depart from Me, you cursed. . . ." And these will go away into everlasting punishment, but the righteous into eternal life. (Matt. 25:31–34, 41, 46)

5. *The kingdom of heaven.* "The King will say to those on His right hand, 'Come, you blessed of My Father, inherit the kingdom prepared for you from the foundation of the world'" (Matt. 25:34).
6. *Hell.* "Then He will also say to those on the left hand, 'Depart from Me, you cursed, into the everlasting fire prepared for the devil and his angels'" (Matt. 25:41).

Willful Inability and Our Need for Christ

Two biblical truths must be understood to properly answer our question, Is God unjust in requiring of man what he is unable to perform? Man's inability is both hereditary and voluntary.

Men love the depravity of their hearts and choose to commit sin and iniquity. Sinners do not sin against their will!

> And this is the condemnation, that the light has come into the world, and men loved darkness rather than light, because their deeds were evil. For everyone practicing evil hates the light and does not come to the light, lest his deeds should be exposed. But he who does the truth comes to the light, that his deeds may be clearly seen, that they have been done in God. (John 3:19-21)

If God did not require what sinners cannot perform, then they would have no need for the Son of God to fulfill all righteousness for them, or for the Holy Spirit to work holiness in them. If we say that God cannot justly require sinners to perform that obedience which they cannot perform, we undermine both the law and the gospel. Because such obedience is precisely what God does require, the powerful operation of the Holy Spirit to conquer the sinner's resistance to God and His will becomes a necessity. Power is necessary to change the sinner's nature, causing him to love the will of God (which is to love the law of God). The power of the Holy Spirit in conversion puts God's laws into the minds of people and writes God's laws on their hearts (Heb. 10:16), thus creating them in Christ Jesus "for good works" (Eph. 2:10). The Spirit's power works in quickening and raising them from the dead, opening their eyes, and calling them "out of darkness into His marvelous light" (1 Peter 2:9).

If God only required what people could do for themselves, then all that He does for them in Christ would be unnecessary. Inasmuch as the commandments are beyond our ability, they show the fullness and suitableness of the promises of the gospel. God did not give the commandments to man after the Fall with the expectation that we had the ability to keep them. Rather, they were given to convict us of our helplessness and inability to keep them, and thereby to cause us to cast ourselves on God's mercy and seek His grace and forgiveness. And He will never be sought in vain.

The fact that we cannot keep the commandments is no surprise to God. He perfectly knows our inability, and the man who feels his own inability is fully encouraged to depend upon the power of the Savior. This brings together the supreme authority of the Lawgiver and the total insufficiency of the creature. It unites the full provision of the Savior and the all-sufficiency of the grace of God.

- We pray to God for what we lack.
- We are thankful to God for what we have.
- We trust God for what He has promised.

If God were to reduce our duty and make it commensurate to our ability, it would mean that the weaker we are, the less is our obligation; and the more sinful we are, the less is required of us.

Those who reject the law because man has no power to keep it seem to forget that they have no power even to believe the gospel. The command to believe is just as impossible for the natural man as the command to obey. The absence of ability does not imply absence of obligation in either case (John 6:44).

God's Commands and Human Inability

The gospel command "Believe on the Lord Jesus Christ and you shall be saved" is addressed by divine authority to all people. It is their duty. Some deny this on the ground that man lacks the spiritual ability to believe in Jesus. But it is wrong to imagine that the measure of the sinner's moral duty is his ability.

There are many things that people ought to do but have lost the moral and spiritual power to do. They ought to be chaste; but, if someone has been immoral so long that he cannot restrain his passions, he is not therefore freed from that obligation. It is the duty of a debtor to pay his debts; if, however, he has been such a spendthrift that he has brought himself into hopeless poverty, he is not thereby exonerated from his debts. Every man ought to believe what is true; but, if his mind has become so depraved that he loves a lie and will not receive the truth, is he thereby excused?

If the law of God were lowered to the moral condition of sinners, it would become a sliding scale to suit their degrees of human sinfulness. In fact, the worst man would be under the least obligation and become the least guilty. If God's requirements were variable, we would be under no rule at all.

The commandments of God stand, regardless of how bad men may be. When He commands all men everywhere to repent, they are bound to repent whether their sinfulness renders their wills unable to do so or not. In every case, it is man's duty to do what God commands him.

What kind of God would He be to keep lowering the standard of what is right because men do not and cannot, in their own strength, do what is required? That would be like painting the bull's eye around the arrow regardless of where it lands.

A man cannot satisfy a bond by breach of contract. Nor does a person by breaking the law free himself from the law's demands. Likewise, God does not take a man's failing in his duty as reason to excuse him from performing that duty. God has not lost His right to command those who have lost their ability to perform. The sinner's impotency does not dissolve his obligation.

Someone might say, "He who commands impossibilities commands in vain; therefore, the commands since the Fall are in vain." But God does not command in vain (even when we fail to perform what He requires of us); His commands have other uses and purposes, in respect to both the righteous and the wicked.

It is manifest that the very best actions of the unconverted are sinful in the sight of God. "The plowing of the wicked [is] sin" (Prov. 21:4). Such persons may indeed do many things that are materially good, but nothing that is spiritually good: done from a good principle, in a good manner, and to a good end. All that they do is either directly or indirectly in opposition to the holy commandments of the Lord, and so it is sinful and hateful to Him (Prov. 15:8). How, then, can such performances atone for their past transgressions and entitle them to the favor of God and eternal life? How deep is the infatuation, and how great the folly, of relying on our own righteousness for a title to eternal salvation!

From what I have said, it is also evident that it is a righteous thing for God to require of unregenerate sinners what they cannot perform. He commands them to love Him with all their hearts and to perform perfect and perpetual obedience to His righteous law. In their unregenerate state, however, they have no moral ability to perform a single duty according to the commandments (Rom. 5:6). It is, nonetheless, infinitely just that the Lord should require of sinners what they are unwilling and unable to perform.

Likewise, it is right that He should condemn them to death for not performing the full extent of the law. For nothing can be more just and reasonable than that men should yield perfect obedience to His righteous law. He gave commandments to our first parents and sufficient ability to perform perfect obedience (Eccl. 7:29). Yet, they chose to deprive themselves of it by their transgression as the federal representatives of the whole human race (Rom. 5:12, 19). Furthermore, people have no excuse for what is voluntary. They love the depravity of their hearts, and choose to commit iniquity.

Human Inability and Spiritual Power

As we have seen, if the Lord could not justly require of sinners what they cannot perform, it would inevitably follow that they would have no need either for the Son of God to fulfill all righteousness for them or for His Holy Spirit to implant holiness in them. Therefore, to say that God cannot justly require sinners to perform obedience that, of themselves, they are unable to perform, tends to undermine both the law and the gospel.

We can also see that no influence of the Holy Spirit but that which is irresistible will suffice to convert a sinner to God and to the love and practice of sincere obedience to His law. So strong is the corruption in the hearts of the unregenerate that even the elect resist the saving operation of the Spirit for a time.

If the Spirit were not infinitely efficacious in His work, they would resist His converting them. An infinitely powerful operation of the Holy Spirit, sufficient to conquer the full resistance of sinners, is necessary to change their nature and to make them willing to believe in Jesus Christ and return to the Lord. Accordingly, the Holy Spirit in converting sinners is represented in Scripture as putting His laws into their minds and writing them in their hearts, creating them in Christ Jesus for good works, quickening and raising them up from the dead, and calling them out of darkness into His marvelous light.

We cannot think of men receiving the gospel, with all its promises of mercy and forgiveness, apart from the Spirit of God. Without Him, the gospel would achieve nothing. By itself the gospel would be as much a dead letter as the law. But neither the law nor the gospel is a dead letter because the Holy Spirit uses both in saving and sanctifying His people (Rom. 8:4).

Hence, they are said to be born of the Spirit, to be new creatures, and to walk in newness of life. This great and wonderful change is indispensable to true conversion. Happy are you if you have experienced this marvelous change! As soon as you do, you begin to believe the gospel, to commune with the Second Adam in His righteousness and salvation, and to obey His law, growing in "a walk worthy of the Lord, fully pleasing Him" (Col. 1:10).

CHAPTER TEN

God's Law and God's Love

"If you love Me, keep My commandments." (John 14:15)

"This is the love of God, that we keep His commandments. And His commandments are not burdensome." (1 John 5:3)

What God Has Joined

In order to serve the Lord faithfully, we must not only distinguish things that differ but also preserve the connection of things God has joined. Law and love are two such things that God has joined. They are inseparable mates.

When Martin Luther said, "Love God and do as you please," his point was this: If you truly love God, you will do what pleases *Him*. But that still leaves the question, What is pleasing to God? Thus Luther's statement needs some explanation, lest the issue be oversimplified or confused.

One of the greatest difficulties in dealing with this subject is the many ways the words themselves, *law* and *love*, are used in the Bible. In chapter 6 we discussed the different meanings of the word *law*. Likewise, in Scripture we read of the love of Christ, love for your wife, love for our neighbor, love for our enemies, and a special and peculiar love for the brethren. Volumes have been written on these two little words, *law* and *love*.

Every true Christian wants to know how to please God. This desire comes with the new birth and immediately thrusts us into the Bible, where God's will is expressed. But how does God express His will? Does He simply say, "Love . . ." or does He express His will by giving us His commandments? The Bible clearly does both, all the while teaching us the proper relationship between law and love.

We must exercise our best efforts to discern what that relationship is. The assortment of books, discussions, and opinions on this subject is vast. Thus sorting through the issues requires prayer and the plentiful work of the Holy Spirit, the only true Teacher. May God give us all discernment to distinguish things that differ and to join things that must be understood together.

"All You Need Is Love"?

Every heresy and cult waves the word *love* around like a banner of virtue. It is their favorite word, but it is never connected to God's law. The hippie movement of the sixties also proclaimed this word—painted on vans and placards—often in the form of "free love." Political liberals continue to speak of love divorced from individual responsibility.

In March of 1965, *Time* magazine reported a meeting of nine hundred ministers and students at Harvard Divinity School in which they considered the subject of the "new morality." The title of the article, "Love in Place of Law?" set up an antithesis. Under the heading, "We Are Delivered," the article said, "Inevitably, the speakers reached no definite conclusion, but they generally agreed, that, in some respects, the new morality is a healthy advance as a genuine effort to take literally St. Paul's teaching that through Christ we are delivered from the law."

Though these words do come from the New Testament, they certainly do not teach what the Harvard speakers implied. Some questions need to be asked about the context of Paul's words: In what respect are we delivered from the law, and, from what laws are we delivered? People who are motivated by genuine love are certainly not lawless. They love the moral and ethical standard that Christ loved and kept, contrary to the words of Princeton president, Paul Ramsey, who said in the same article, "Lists of cans and cannots are meaningless."

Now, we are not surprised at this dangerous, destructive ig-norance when we find it among cults, liberals, and agnostics. But when Bible-believing preachers set up a false antithesis be-tween law and love, we should be shocked, appalled, sad-dened, and greatly pained.

Setting up a false antithesis between law and love (as if they are conflicting, opposing ideas) is one of the most subtle ways to undermine the Ten Commandments, biblical morality, and true Christianity. Granted there is a difference between law and love; but there is also an immutable connection. The failure to see this unchangeable relationship has led people into count-less errors, heresies, and spiritual shipwrecks.

An Immutable Connection

Let us consider a few passages that show the immutable con-nection between law and love. Notice how love is joined to the Ten Commandments in the following teaching of Paul:

> Owe no one anything except to love one another, for he who loves another has fulfilled the law. For the com-mandments, "You shall not commit adultery," "You shall not murder," "You shall not steal," "You shall not bear false witness," "You shall not covet," and if there is any other commandment, are all summed up in this saying, namely, "You shall love your neighbor as your-self." Love does no harm to a neighbor; therefore love is the fulfillment of the law. (Rom. 13:8–10)

Moreover, what better definition of love could we give than the biblical one we have from John, the great apostle of love himself? "For this is the love of God, that we keep His com-mandments. And His commandments are not burdensome" (1 John 5:3).

Observe, also, our Lord's conversation with the lawyer in Matthew 22:35-40. When asked in verse 36, "Teacher, which is the great commandment in the law?" our Lord immediately connected God's commandments and God's love. Jesus always connected law and love. What could be plainer than the following examples?

> He who has My commandments and keeps them, it is he who loves Me. And he who loves Me will be loved by My Father, and I will love him and manifest Myself to him. . . . If anyone loves Me, he will keep My word; and My Father will love him, and We will come to him and make Our home with him. He who does not love Me does not keep My words; and the word which you hear is not Mine but the Father's who sent Me." (John 14:21, 23-24)

> If you keep My commandments, you will abide in My love, just as I have kept My Father's commandments and abide in His love. . . . This is My commandment, that you love one another as I have loved you. . . . You are My friends if you do whatever I command you." (John 15:10, 12, 14)

These statements should settle forever the fact that there is an eternal relationship between God's law and God's love.

To emphasize that love itself is a command is consistent with many New Testament passages: "Love your neighbor" (Matt. 5:43); "love your enemies" (Luke 6:27, 35); "love one another" (Rom. 13:8); "love your wives" (Eph. 5:25); "love the brotherhood" (1 Peter 2:17).

These passages are sufficiently clear to show that there is a vital connection between law and love. They should cause us to renounce any teaching—whether packaged in clever illustrations or dispensed via subtle implications—that would separate law and love. If ever the biblical teaching about the commandments was needed in the home, the church, and the nation, it is now! With lawlessness rampant, we certainly do not need preachers and teachers who separate what God has joined together.

The "love only" doctrine is the enemy of true Christianity, of the Bible, and of the souls of men. It is not biblical love at all. Nor is lawless love Christlike.

The gospel of Christ breathes the Spirit of holy love, namely:

- Love is the fulfilling of all gospel precepts.
- Love is the pledge of all gospel joys.
- Love is the evidence of gospel power.
- Love is the ripe fruit of the Spirit (Gal. 5:22-23).

The Spirit of genuine love is never, never, at the expense of law and truth. Nor is love ever separated from the biblical directives for holy living that are objectively and eternally set out in the Ten Commandments. This is underscored in that great love chapter in the Bible, where Paul says that "love rejoices in the truth" (1 Cor. 13:6).

The connection between law and love is deeply embedded in the Old Testament, as well as the New. This is illustrated in Exodus 20, where God gave the Decalogue at Sinai. Before giving the Ten Commandments, God reminded the Israelites of His redemptive love. "I am the LORD your God, who brought you out of the land of Egypt" (v. 2). That was a loving redemptive act. Not only does the prologue to the Ten Commandments speak of God's redeeming love, but later, in reference to the second commandment, verse 6 speaks of God's "showing mercy" to His people. Love and mercy are harmoniously tied to the Decalogue.

Jesus reaffirmed that connection in John 14:15: "If you love Me, keep My commandments." His summary of the law in Matthew 22:37-40—the law of love for God and neighbor— echoes the love command given with the law in Deuteronomy 6:5. Not only our Lord and His apostle, but the whole Bible joins God's law and God's love.

Love as Motive

Love has no eyes except the holy law of God, no direction apart from God's commands. Paul spoke of the love of Christ con-

straining us. It moves us to duty. Love is the only true motive
for all worship and duty, but by itself it does not define either.
Therefore, we may not put love "in place of law." They belong
together. Christian behavior springs from love to God and our
neighbor. If we loved them perfectly, our character and behavior would be perfect because it would conform to God's will.
Love is a motive for and expresses itself in obedient action.

Such action fulfills the law: "Love does no harm to a neighbor; therefore love is the fulfillment of the law" (Rom. 13:10).
Motive and action cannot be more tightly joined than they are
in this passage. If love does not constrain us to fulfill the moral
law, it is not the love of which the Bible speaks. The apostle Paul
made this very clear when he said that "the love of Christ constrains us" (2 Cor. 5:14). It is the love of God that puts the law
of God into effect.

Genuine love for God is intensely preoccupied with Him as
the Supreme Object of love. It is, therefore, intrinsically active
in doing His will. Love itself is commanded in the Old Testament as well as the New. Jesus said, "These things I command
you, that you love one another" (John 15:17). Love is also described as a command in Deuteronomy 6:5-7: "You shall love
the LORD your God with all your heart, with all your soul, and
with all your might. And these words which I command you
today shall be in your heart; you shall teach them diligently to
your children, and shall talk of them when you sit in your
house, when you walk by the way, when you lie down, and
when you rise up."

We must be very clear that the command to love will not create love or generate love. This command, like every other, cannot create the disposition or will to obey. But the mere fact that
love is a command should silence those who argue for an antithesis between law and love. Moses, Jesus, and Paul all connected law and love, as does John in 1 John 5:3: "For this is the
love of God, that we keep His commandments. And His commandments are not burdensome."

Woe to anyone who separates what Moses, Christ, and the
apostles have said belong together! What God has joined let no
man put asunder.

Law Defines Love

The full content and direction of the law is not defined by love. When the Bible speaks of the "law of love," it cannot mean that love stands by itself as a definition of righteousness. Love is a principle of action, just as Paul, speaking of our remaining sin, describes that sin as a law or principle of action: "I find then a law, that, when I would do good, evil is present with me. . . . But I see another law in my members, warring against the law of my mind, and bringing me into captivity to the law of sin which is in my members" (Rom. 7:21, 23 KJV). As a principle of action, law directs us in the true expression of love. Love does not spontaneously follow its own way. It is the fulfilling of the law. The law is love's eyes, without which love is blind.

Realizing this proper connection between law and love will drive us to all of Scripture to discover the behavior that God clearly defines as loving obedience. Nowhere in the Scriptures will we find that love dictates its own standard of conduct. We hear our Lord say, "If you love Me, keep My commandments," not, "If you love me, love me in any way you feel."

> He who has My commandments and keeps them, it is he who loves Me. And he who loves Me will be loved by My Father, and I will love him and manifest Myself to him. (John 14:21)

> If you keep My commandments, you will abide in My love, just as I have kept My Father's commandments and abide in His love. (John 15:10)

Our Lord's commandments in respect to morality are no different from His Father's commands. Otherwise there would be war in the Trinity. (Our difficulties in understanding the Trinity are immense enough without our suggesting a division in the Trinity!) There are not two moral standards of righteousness in the Bible—Christ's and the Father's. Nor is the Bible divided against itself, such that Old Testament believers were directed by law, but New Testament believers are directed by love.

Biblical love is never an autonomous, self-directing force capable of defining its own norms or standards of behavior. It is the fulfilling of God's commandments. We must not subtract love from the whole context of biblical revelation. Love does not stand alone or act alone. It has many biblical relatives, and the law is one of them.

A Heart for the Law

Likewise, the true Christian does not let his own heart—even though it is a renewed heart—spontaneously decide what is right. That heart must be directed by God's law. Indeed, the Spirit writes the law on the hearts and minds of all who are born again (Heb. 8:10; 10:16).

Does that mean that we come to know the law simply by reading an inscription on our hearts? No. The teaching of Hebrews 8:10 and 10:16 is that the renewed heart has an affinity with, and love for, the law of God, resulting in cheerful, loving obedience. "For this is the love of God, that we keep His commandments. And His commandments are not burdensome" (1 John 5:3). "I delight in the law of God" (Rom. 7:22). Here again we see an important bond between God's law and love.

If fallen man has the work of the law written on his heart so that he does by nature the things of the law (Rom. 2:14–15), how much clearer it must have been written on Adam's heart in his original state! And if the renewed man has the law written upon his heart, surely it cannot be different in principle from what was first written on Adam's heart and later written on tables of stone at Sinai.

Scripture dispels that ignorant, erroneous idea that love is its own law and the renewed conscience its own monitor. And yet, this wicked fancy continues to abound among Bible teachers, despite the clear testimony of Scriptures to the contrary.

I recently read an article by a brilliant young author who was busily sowing the seeds of antinomianism. In the article, he raised a question about sexual purity: "What perspective does

Paul press on the Corinthians to dissuade them from sexual immorality?" (The author was referring to 1 Cor. 6:18-20, where the apostle tells the Corinthians to "flee fornication.") The young writer answered his own question: "The death of Christ by which they were purchased." What the author failed to consider, however, was how Paul or the Corinthians knew what sexual immorality was. How did they know—and how can we know—what constituted sexually immorality?

It is one thing to use the death of Christ, whereby they were purchased, as a motive for obedience to flee fornication. It is another thing to know and understand our duty to be chaste. The duty is not found in the word *love*. It is found in the seventh commandment.

The same author noted that "obedience flows from the redemptive work of Christ." Surely a proper motive for obedience is our gratitude for Jesus' redeeming work. But there must also be an objective standard for obedience before we can understand how to obey. *Motive* is one thing—specific *duty* is another. They are different, though vitally related.

Shouting "Love!" (the motive) tells us nothing specifically about our moral duties. The proper expressions of love are defined by the commandments of God. Though the Christian life is not initiated or sustained by commandment or law, Christian duty has no definition or direction without divine law.

When Paul says in Romans 13:9–10 that the commandments are summarized by the law of love, his point is not that love replaces law or is exempt from it. Law is not abrogated by love; it is fulfilled. Love neither supersedes law nor releases us from obedience. It enables us to obey. Love does not make stealing or coveting, or any breach of the law, something other than sin for the Christian (though some would give this passage that meaning). Love so penetrates and so constrains us that (not reluctantly or through fear, but joyfully) we act toward our neighbor in all things, great and small, as the law bids us. Yes, Christ has redeemed us from the curse of the law, but not from the law itself. That would be to redeem us from a divine rule and guide, from that which is "holy, and just, and good."

Love as "a New Commandment"—John 13:34

An often misused text of Scripture is John 13:34, where Jesus says: "A new commandment I give to you, that you love one another; as I have loved you, that you also love one another." Does this verse imply that a new law—the law of love—has replaced the older Ten Commandments? Is that what Jesus meant when He spoke of "a new commandment"?

To understand this verse, or any verse, we must first examine it in its immediate context and in its remote context. But before doing that, it would be helpful to remind ourselves of some principles for interpreting Scripture.

Interpreting Scripture
In the very first chapter of The Westminster Confession of Faith, we have a rule of interpretation.

> The infallible rule of interpretation of scripture is the scripture itself; and therefore, when there is a question about the true and full sense of any scripture, (which is not manifold, but one) it may be searched and known by other places that speak more clearly. (1.10)

This rule has been called the "analogy of Scripture" or the "analogy of faith." Its meaning and importance have been well stated by Charles Hodge.

> If the Scriptures be what they claim to be, the word of God, they are the work of one mind, and that mind divine. From this it follows that Scripture cannot contradict Scripture. God cannot teach in one place anything which is inconsistent with what He teaches in another. Hence Scripture must explain Scripture. (*Systematic Theology* [Grand Rapids: Eerdmans, 1952], 187)

No doctrine concerning Scripture is of more importance to the Bible student than that which affirms its unity and harmony. From that principle flow the following rules for interpreting Scripture:

1. When the plain sense of Scripture is clear, seek no other sense; therefore, take every work at its usual, literal, primary meaning unless the context dictates otherwise.
2. Subordinate passages must always be interpreted in the light of leading truths.
3. What is obscure must be interpreted by the light of what is plain. Peripheral ambiguities must be interpreted in harmony with fundamental certainties. No interpretation of any text, therefore, is right which does not agree with the principles of religion, the Apostles' Creed, the Lord's Prayer, and the Ten Commandments.

In addition, if you have only one passage of Scripture on which to form some important doctrine, you will probably find, on closer examination, that you have none.

With these reminders before us, let us examine John 13:34: "A new commandment I give to you, that you love one another."

The Context of John 13:34

John 13:34 is part of our Lord's lesson on servanthood. He illustrates this concept by washing the disciples' feet (13:3–16). *Nowhere* in this entire chapter is our Lord giving a code of moral conduct or an objective standard of righteousness. That is not His subject in John 13. Therefore, we must be careful not to ask of *this* verse, What is the biblical standard of moral conduct? Love is the answer, *but not to that question;* which is to say, that is not the question raised here. To answer "love" to that question may sound very pious, but we would still need to define "love." How does Christian love act? In what direction does love go? How does love manifest itself toward God and man?

John 13 does not tell us those things. It does not teach us that we are to worship God; or that we are not to steal, murder, or commit adultery; or that we are to honor our father and mother.

Our Lord's subject instead is "servanthood," and the key to verse 34 is found in the words, "as I have loved you." These words take us to the supreme example—the suffering servant—and that takes us to the cross.

A cross without a broken law is a cross without sin. Without law and sin, the cross is a jig-saw puzzle with the key pieces missing. Basic to the cross is Christ's satisfying divine justice, thereby upholding the law. The spirit of the cross is His manifesting saving love. The cross affirms law and love together. Verse 35 says, "By this all men will know that you are My disciples, if you have love for one another." Does this mean that all men know that we are His disciples if we march around holding up "Love" signs, or singing "Love, love, love"? Of course not! They will know that we follow Christ if they see Christlike love in our actions—holy deeds of mercy as defined by the Father's commands.

To follow Jesus' example is to love what Jesus loved, and to hate what Jesus hated, conforming our conduct to the same standard that He perfectly obeyed. He could say, "I do not seek My own will but the will of the Father who sent Me" (John 5:30). Where is the Father's will expressed in respect to morals? In the holy commands of Scripture. Jesus was indeed a law-keeping Savior.

Was the Command to Love New?

Was the command in John 13:34—to "love one another"—new? No, the law of love for God and man is the summary of all the commandments, and has been from the giving of the law to Moses.

> Hear, O Israel: The LORD our God, the LORD is one! *You shall love the LORD your God with all your heart, with all your soul, and with all your might.* And these words which I command you today shall be in your heart; you shall teach them diligently to your children, and shall talk of them when you sit in your house, when you walk by the way, when you lie down, and when you rise up. You

shall bind them as a sign on your hand, and they shall
be as frontlets between your eyes. You shall write them
on the doorposts of your house and on your gates.
(Deut. 6:4-9)

You shall not take vengeance, nor bear any grudge
against the children of your people, but *you shall love
your neighbor as yourself*: I am the LORD. (Lev. 19:18)

Then one of them, a lawyer, asked Him a question, test-
ing Him, and saying, "Teacher, which is the great commandment in the law?" Jesus said to him, "'*You shall
love the LORD your God with all your heart, with all your
soul, and with all your mind.*' This is the first and great
commandment. And the second is like it: '*You shall love
your neighbor as yourself.*' On these two commandments
hang all the Law and the Prophets." (Matt. 22:35-40)

These passages, and many more, prove conclusively that to
love is not a new obligation. Nor is it a new, different standard
of right conduct. There already was a perfect, eternal standard
of morality in the Ten Commandments, which has always been
summarized by the law of love.

What Was New About the Command to Love?
What was new about our Lord's command in John 13:34? The
answer is in the words "as I have loved you." The text offers a
living demonstration of servanthood. In the person and work
of Jesus, love was manifested, yes, personified, as never before!
Our Lord displayed:

- a love superior to its objects.
- a love that never varied.
- a love that deemed no sacrifice too great. He gave *Himself*. "Greater love has no one than this, than to lay down
  one's life for his friends" (John 15:13).
- a love that did not subordinate, abrogate, or mitigate the
  law.

The love that Christ explained and manifested had always been commanded but never so pointedly demonstrated or personified. Such a demonstration was new! This commandment was also new in respect to its objects. God's new commandment was *brotherly* love, "that you love one another." *Brotherly* love is a special kind of love, going beyond love for one's neighbor. It is intended for a special people—the people of God.

> Brethren, I write no new commandment to you, but an old commandment which you have had from the beginning. The old commandment is the word which you heard from the beginning. Again, a new commandment I write to you . . . because the darkness is passing away, and the true light is already shining. He who says he is in the light, and hates his *brother*, is in the darkness until now. He who loves his *brother*, abides in the light, and there is no cause for stumbling in him. But he who hates his *brother* is in darkness and walks in darkness, and does not know where he is going, because the darkness has blinded his eyes. (1 John 2:7–11)

Brotherly love regarding the family of God is a new dimension to an old commandment. The commandment is new in respect to its manifestation of servanthood and new in respect to the objects of this love. Not only are we to have kind affections toward all men—that is just plain Christian benevolence. And genuine love to neighbors is extended to all according to their circumstances. We are even instructed to love our enemies. But this is not *"brotherly love."*

Brotherly love—the love of godly men and women for their godliness—is peculiar to the household of faith. An affection directed toward the excellency of true religion, it delights in holiness and truth. It loves the image of God reflected in God's true sons and daughters. This love attracts the eye and wins the heart because it embraces that divine nature of born-again men and women.

God imparts to His own a portion of His own loveliness. He

has made them new creatures of His free and distinguishing grace. Christ loves them as His own, calling them "My sheep." The Holy Spirit loves them, and they love each other. To love Christ is to love those who are like Him. Among His people, all divisions vanish: name and nation, rank and party, race and gender. All are lost in the common name Christian. Jew and Gentile, bond and free, rich and poor, male and female are one in Christ. We have one Lord, one faith, one baptism (Eph. 4:5).

It is by the mark of brotherly love that Jesus' disciples are to judge themselves. "We know that we have passed from death to life, because we love the brethren" (1 John 3:14). This is also the criterion by which Christ would have the world judge the sincerity of His religion and the truth of His gospel. "By this all will know that you are My disciples, if you have love for one another" (John 13:35).

THIS NEW BROTHERLY LOVE does not negate the objective standard of the Ten Commandments. It applies the commandments in a fresh and compelling way to the communion of the saints. Love and law, working together, give us clear guidance in how to please God and know His will. The law shows us our sin and thrusts us to the cross and the Savior for mercy and grace. Love constrains us to walk a path of righteousness defined by the commandments and marked by joy and humble servanthood. That is the right relationship between law and love.

CHAPTER ELEVEN

The Law and the Savior

*"Do not think that I came to destroy the Law
or the Prophets. I did not come to destroy
but to fulfill." (Matt. 5:17)*

THE SERMON ON THE MOUNT (Matt. 5-7) expresses our Lord's
relationship to the law. Any careful study of this sermon of all
sermons should conclude that Jesus was not abrogating or
changing the moral standard of righteousness. That is clear
from His words in Matthew 5:17-20.

> Do not think that I came to destroy the Law or the
> Prophets. I did not come to destroy but to fulfill. "For
> assuredly, I say to you, till heaven and earth pass away,
> one jot or one tittle will by no means pass from the law
> till all is fulfilled. Whoever therefore breaks one of the
> least of these commandments, and teaches men so, shall
> be called least in the kingdom of heaven; but whoever
> does and teaches them, he shall be called great in the
> kingdom of heaven. For I say to you, that unless your
> righteousness exceeds the righteousness of the scribes
> and Pharisees, you will by no means enter the kingdom
> of heaven."

Far from doing away with the law, Jesus is restoring its true
and spiritual meaning, which the scribes and Pharisees have

104

lost. Speaking of the whole Old Testament (apparently) in verse 18, the commandments in verse 19, and His main theme of *righteousness* in 5:20, Jesus draws two important conclusions: (1) He passionately denies that His ethical teaching is in opposition to, or at variance with, the moral system of the Old Testament. His teaching agrees perfectly with the moral commandments of the law and the prophets. (2) He emphasizes that the teaching of the scribes and Pharisees is so erroneous that anyone who does not rise above their ethical standard will surely not enter the kingdom of heaven.

Our Lord's teaching in this immortal sermon does not drive a wedge between the Old and the New Testaments, as many modern teachers do. He did not come to annul, abrogate, improve, destroy, or make void the righteousness of the law and the prophets.

That is further established by the fact that Jesus and His apostles constantly appealed to the Old Testament Scriptures to prove and buttress their teaching. If all the Old Testament quotations were removed from the New Testament, it would be much shorter. (For example, see what would happen if all Old Testament allusions were omitted from the book of Romans, where we have the best of the apostle Paul's theology.)

Jesus did not come to destroy the law. He came to explain it—even to expand its application. That very fact proves that it remains relevant today. Yet, religious teachers continue to stumble over the relationship of Christ and the law, of grace and the law, as did the religious leaders of Jesus' day.

The Scribes' and Pharisees' Misuse of the Law

There were three fundamental ways in which the scribes and Pharisees perverted true religion.

- They were more interested in details than principles.
- They were more interested in outward appearance than inner motives.
- They were more interested in doing than being.

In addressing these errors, Jesus had a perfect opportunity to discard the law had He wanted to. But the remedy to Pharisaic legalism was not to annul the law, for the problem was not the law itself, but its misuse. Jesus answers this distortion of the law with five assertions.

- He did not come to destroy the law (v. 17).
- He came to fulfill the law (v. 17).
- The moral law is a perpetual obligation, outlasting heaven and earth (v. 18).
- He who breaks the least of the commandments, and teaches others to do so, shall suffer loss (v. 19).
- He who obeys and teaches others to obey will be rewarded, called great in the kingdom of God (v. 19).

The Law of the Lord Versus Traditions of Men

If Jesus is not opposing the law itself in this sermon, then what problem is He addressing? A very crucial recurring phrase in Matthew 5:21–44 is the words, "You have heard that it was said" or "it has been said," to which Jesus responds, "But I say . . ." (see vv. 21–22; 27-28; 31–32; 33-34; 38-39; 43-44). Notice, the passage does not first say "the commandments say." It does not contrast what the law says with what Jesus says. It contrasts what "you have heard" with what "I say."

Jesus is contrasting the prevalent, erroneous teaching on the law with His true, full understanding of it. Where have the people heard what they have been wrongly taught? They have heard it from religious leaders who are preoccupied with minute details and outward actions, at the expense of central principles, inner motives, and true spirituality.

The scribes and Pharisees were well acquainted with the Old Testament Scriptures. But they had explained the Scriptures away by their traditions. They were so occupied with the mere appearance of godliness that they missed the central point of the revelation given to them: "You search the Scriptures, for in them you think you have eternal life; and these are they which testify of Me. But you are not willing to come to Me that you may have life" (John 5:39-40). That is why Jesus said to them,

> "Well did Isaiah prophesy of you hypocrites, as it is written: 'This people honors Me with their lips, but their heart is far from Me, and in vain they worship Me, teaching as doctrines the commandments of men.' For laying aside the commandment of God, you hold the tradition of men—the washing of pitchers and cups, and many other such things you do." And He said to them, "All too well you reject the commandment of God, that you may keep your tradition." (Mark 7:6-9)

Heart Religion Versus Externalism

What was the problem with the scribes' and Pharisees' interpretation of the commandments? Their basic error was that they missed the meaning of the tenth commandment as it applies to all the others. The tenth commandment deals with the heart, as well as with externals. Exodus 20:17 teaches the internal meaning of the rest of the commandments: "You shall not covet your neighbor's house; you shall not covet your neighbor's wife, nor his manservant, nor his maidservant, nor his ox, nor his donkey, nor anything that is your neighbor's."

Likewise, in Matthew 5:22-46, the Lord is showing that the commandments are more than external. They go to the heart. Christianity is a heart religion, and if the heart is right, the external conduct will be right. After all, where does murder begin? Where does adultery begin? Jesus tells us in Mark 7:21–23: "For from within, out of the heart of men, proceed evil thoughts, adulteries, fornication, murders, thefts, covetousness, wickedness, deceit, licentiousness, an evil eye, blasphemy, pride, foolishness. All these evil things come from within and defile a man."

Jesus is seeking to correct externalism, legalism, and pharisaism. Though the Pharisees knew and taught the law, they missed the fact that the law is spiritual (Rom. 7:14). As we have noted earlier, it was the tenth commandment that revealed

Paul's sin to him and led to his conversion: "I would not have known sin except through the law. For I would not have known covetousness unless the law had said, 'You shall not covet'" (Rom. 7:7).

Throughout Matthew 5 Jesus is seeking to restore the real meaning of the moral law when He says repeatedly, "But I say . . ." (see vv. 22, 28, 32, 34, 39, 44). The law in the hand of Christ has a merciful administration. Jesus' dealings with the adulteress woman in John 8 is a good example of His blending mercy with the law.

Destruction Versus Fulfilling of the Law

We also learn from this passage that Jesus is seeking to correct the false opinions that the religious leaders have concerning His approach to the law: "I did not come to destroy [the law] but to fulfill" (v. 17). By their perverted teaching and slavish attachments to their traditions, the Pharisees have cast Jesus as a deceiver who seeks to overthrow the whole law. They have sought to put questions in peoples' minds, such as: Does He really believe the Scriptures? Is His teaching new? Is He saying that there is some new way to God? Is He turning His back on our past— all our history, our laws, and our traditions? Has He come to do away with the Scriptures and the law?

Jesus counters by appealing to three realities:

- The very purpose of His coming—not to destroy but to fulfill the law (vv. 17–18).
- The very nature of the law—that it will not pass away, though heaven and earth pass away (vv. 18–19).
- The very nature of the kingdom of heaven (v. 19) and the scope of His ministry (v. 20)—true righteousness, not religious sentimentalism or sanctimonious hypocrisy.

Throughout Matthew 5:17-20, two principles come to the foreground: (1) Jesus' teaching is in perfect *harmony* with the Old Testament (vv. 17–18). (2) His teaching is in complete *disharmony* with the teaching of the scribes and Pharisees.

Verses 17–18 begin a new section with the words, "Do not think that I came to destroy the Law and the Prophets. I did not come to destroy but to fulfill. For assuredly, I say to you, till heaven and earth pass away, one jot or one tittle will by no means pass from the law till all is fulfilled." This is one of the most stupendous claims our Lord ever made. Think of it— everything in all the law and all the prophets culminated in Him. In these two verses our Lord puts His seal of authority and His imprimatur on the whole Old Testament.

Verses 17–19 have been the focus of three erroneous views:

- That all Jesus did was to continue the Old Testament duties.
- That He abolished the law completely and brought grace instead of law. The teachers of this error set up an antithesis between the Old and New Testaments—between Moses and Christ.
- That the sermon has nothing to do with Christianity today. It is for the kingdom age. This is the dispensational view—or at least was; dispensationalism is changing so much, like a moving target, that one cannot be quite sure what it teaches.

In order to understand this crucial passage, it is necessary to have a clear idea of what its key terms mean, terms such as *destroy, law, prophets*, and especially *fulfill*.

"Destroy"

From several translations, we learn that "destroy" in verse 17 can mean "dissolve" or "abrogate" or "undo" or "invalidate" or "dishonor." Conversely, "fulfill" can mean "carry out," "fulfill [the law and the prophets] to the full measure of the intent and purpose." The nature of the law's fulfillment, which we shall discuss more fully below, rules out any notion of dissolving, abrogating, or invalidating the law. Jesus' fulfillment of the law constitutes the confirmation of Old Testament revelation—

its validation. Yes, even more, the law finds in Him its embodiment. He is the very embodiment of the righteousness required by the law.

The purpose of Jesus' mission was not to repeal or annul God's standards of righteousness, or to improve upon the Ten Commandments. Nor did He come to lessen their authority or to free men from the obligations of obeying them.

If Jesus has not destroyed the law, then the law still stands with all of its divine authority. And if the law still abides as the unchanged expression of God's character and will, then every creature under heaven is under lasting obligation to obey it. When someone becomes a new creature in Christ, he or she does not cease to be a creature under the moral law. And if our Lord did not destroy the law, beware of preachers who seek to destroy or pervert it.

"The Law" and "the Prophets"

What is meant by "the Law" and "the Prophets"? In short, the whole Old Testament. The term "Prophets" clearly means all that we have in the prophetic books of the Old Testament. Two important aspects of the prophetic books is that they themselves proclaim the law, and they interpret and apply it.

The word "Law" in this particular place seems to refer to the entire legal code given to the children of Israel, consisting of three parts: the moral, the judicial, and the ceremonial. Because we discussed these in chapter 6 and will come back to them later in this chapter, we need only summarize the differences between them here.

The moral law consists of the Ten Commandments and the great moral principles laid down once and forever to all creatures (including all "new creatures") of all ages. It will never be abrogated, abolished, or done away with.

The judicial or civil laws were given to the nation of Israel as a theocracy. They were peculiar to the circumstances of Israel at the time and taught men how they were to order their behavior in their relationship to others. To a great degree these laws were an application of the Ten Commandments to one's neighbor (particularly, the second table of the law).

The ceremonial law had to do with the religious worship of Old Testament Israel—their rituals, ceremonies, offerings, sacrifices. These laws prefigured Christ, as we see in Hebrews 9–10.

When our Lord said that He came to fulfill the law, it included all laws. Our Lord is here referring to everything that the law teaches about worship, life, conduct, and behavior. From Matthew 5:21 onward, our Lord is speaking, in particular, of the moral law only.

"Fulfill"

This brings us to the very important word "fulfill," the purpose for which Christ came to earth in reference to the law. There is no small amount of difference among respected Bible teachers concerning the meaning of this word. Because of its vital importance, it warrants our full attention.

This word "fulfill" in this context means a great many things:

- To obey the precepts of the moral law in its conventional form.
- To endure the curse of the Lord's people.
- To verify the various types and figures of the ceremonial law.
- To introduce that spiritual system of government of which the judicial law was an emblem.
- To accomplish all the various predictions in the prophets respecting the Messiah (Luke 24:44).

All of this is true, but it is not the whole truth. There is also a sense in which Jesus came to complete the revelation. How did Christ fulfill the whole law in these ways? How did He, for example, fulfill the moral law, the judicial law, and the ceremonial law? And how does He fulfill the law for all men, both believers and unbelievers?

First of all, the law was unfulfilled apart from Christ, as the New Testament teaches us. The law is empty whenever it is separated from Christ. Thus, His very coming—His presence among us—was one way in which He fulfilled the law. He was the goal and embodiment of the law, without whom the graciousness and beauty of the law would not have been realized. That is John's point in the opening chapter of his gospel, where he says, "For the law was given through Moses, but grace and truth came through Jesus Christ" (John 1:17).

The contrast here is not between law and grace, or between Moses and Christ, but between the *period* of Moses and the *period* of Christ. It is a great stumbling block to expect from the law what we can only obtain through Christ. If you separate the law from Christ, nothing fills the void. That is why Paul says in Colossian 2:17 that the law is "a shadow of things to come, but the substance is of Christ." The law came by Moses as the shadow; the substance—the fulfillment of the law—came in Jesus Christ.

And so, He fulfilled the law by His very presence among us. "When the fullness of the time had come, God sent forth His Son, born of a woman, born under the law" (Gal. 4:4). He was born under the law in order to fulfill it by His personal obedience.

Jesus also fulfills the law by His exposition of it in Matthew 5:21–48. There He brings out of the Word of God what the Spirit has put into the Word of God.

Moreover, He fulfills the law in the sense of accepting the penalty of lawbreakers. The apostle Paul speaks of that penalty—God's curse—in Galatians 3:10–14.

> For as many as are of the works of the law are under the curse; for it is written, "Cursed is everyone who does not continue in all things which are written in the book of the law, to do them." But that no one is justified by the law in the sight of God is evident, for "The just shall live by faith." Yet the law is not of faith, but "The man who does them shall live by them." Christ has redeemed us from the curse of the law, having become a

curse for us, (for it is written, "Cursed is everyone who hangs on a tree") that the blessing of Abraham might come upon the Gentiles in Christ Jesus, that we might receive the promise of the Spirit through faith.

In that sense Jesus was under the law, having made Himself subject to its penalty. This, of course, is the point of His discussion with John the Baptist in Matthew 3:13–15: "Then Jesus came from Galilee to John at the Jordan to be baptized by him. And John tried to prevent Him, saying, 'I have need to be baptized by You, and are You coming to me?' But Jesus answered and said to him, 'Permit it to be so now, for thus it is fitting for us to fulfill all righteousness.' Then he allowed Him."

Jesus was symbolically fulfilling all righteousness in His baptism. His baptism with water pointed forward to His baptism in blood upon the cross, by which He fulfilled the penalties of a broken law. Thus, you cannot separate the law from the cross, or the law from the One who hung upon the cross.

Clarifying what "fulfill" does *not* mean will help us to understand what it does mean.

- It does not mean to complete or finish the law.
- It does not mean to add to something that has already begun. The idea is not that the Old Testament began certain moral teachings, carrying them only so far, and then our Lord came on the historic scene to carry the law a stage further, concluding its use as He fulfilled it.
- It certainly does not mean that Christ was a new Lawgiver in place of Moses, or that He gave us a moral law that would supersede and replace the law given by Moses. That law was already perfect, and you cannot supersede absolute perfection (Ps. 19:7). Christ was not a new Lawgiver. He was a law-fulfiller. Nowhere in the New (or Old) Testament is He referred to as a new Lawgiver. There is no such thing as an old moral law and a new moral law; there is one eternal standard of righteousness summarized in the Ten Commandments.

- "Fulfill" does not mean that our Lord is giving us a higher standard of the law than we have in the Ten Commandments.

To fulfill the law is to carry it out, to give full obedience to it, literally carrying out everything that has been said and stated in the law and the prophets. God's absolute moral standards can never be changed or modified to the slightest extent. The law's moral demands are permanent, absolute, and eternal and can never be abrogated or reduced "till heaven and earth pass" (Matt. 5:18).

Our Lord rendered perfect, personal, and perpetual obedience to all of the law's precepts. That is why we can say He was perfect. He obeyed the law from within His heart. With the psalmist, He could say to the Father, "I delight to do Your will, O my God" (Ps. 40:8). Likewise, He could say, "I have come down from heaven, not to do My own will, but the will of Him who sent Me" (John 6:38). In His work on the cross, He fulfilled the prophecy of Isaiah 42:21: "He will magnify the law and make it honorable."

Fulfilled and Yet Perpetual

In Matthew 5:18, Jesus emphasizes that "till heaven and earth pass away, one jot or one tittle will by no means pass from the law till all is fulfilled." He thereby announces the perpetuity of the law.

In view of the law's continuing authority, it is extremely important that we not confuse law keeping with self-justification. The Bible says, "By the deeds of the law no flesh will be justified" (Rom. 3:20). A man is justified by faith, not by the deeds of the law (Gal. 3:11).

It is here that many go astray. Their reasoning is something like this: If the law serves no purpose in effecting the salvation of sinners, has it no use at all? If we are saved "by faith," is the law useless? Does Paul teach us that the law is annulled and abrogated? Let him answer: "Do we then make void the law through faith? Certainly not! On the contrary, we establish the law" (Rom. 3:31).

Similarly, A. W. Pink addresses the question, If a man is justified by faith, does that not do away with the law entirely and thus teach lawlessness? "By no means. It establishes the law. When a sinner is saved by grace that does not make him lawless. There is a power within him which does not destroy, but strengthens the law, and causes him to love the law and have a desire to keep it, not through fear, but through love of God" (*The Law and the Saint* [Pensacola, Fla.: Chapel Library, n.d.], 27).

The perpetuity of the law is undeniable, but we must not forget Paul's argument in Romans 3.

> But now the righteousness of God apart from the law is revealed, being witnessed by the Law and the Prophets, even the righteousness of God which is through faith in Jesus Christ to all and on all who believe. For there is no difference; for all have sinned and fall short of the glory of God, being justified freely by His grace through the redemption that is in Christ Jesus, whom God set forth to be a propitiation by His blood, through faith, to demonstrate His righteousness, because in His forbearance God had passed over the sins that were previously committed, to demonstrate at the present time His righteousness, that He might be just and the justifier of the one who has faith in Jesus. (vv. 21–26)

The apostle sets forth the divine way of salvation—"through faith in Christ's blood." He sums up his argument by saying that "a man is justified by faith apart from the deeds of the law" (v. 28). Therefore, lawlessness does not reign, but neither are we made right with God through the keeping of the law.

Fulfillment of Three Kinds of Laws
Earlier in this chapter we mentioned three different kinds of laws: judicial or civil, ceremonial, and moral. How did Christ fulfill these different kinds of laws?

The judicial law—civil laws peculiar to the nation of Israel as a theocracy, which were somewhat of an application of the Ten

Commandments: Jesus said, "The kingdom of God will be taken from you and given to a nation bearing the fruits of it" (Matt. 21:43). First Peter 2:9–10, speaking of Jewish and gentile Christians, says, "You are a chosen generation, a royal priesthood, a holy nation, His own special people . . . who once were not a people but are now the people of God."

Jesus fulfilled the civil or judicial law by breaking down the middle wall of partition between Jews and Gentiles (Eph. 2:14). Now they are one in Christ. No one is to be excluded on ethnic grounds.

Jesus also fulfilled the judicial law by obeying the principles embodied in it insofar as they were applications of the Ten Commandments. If anyone is in Christ, he cannot be judged or condemned for failure to keep the judicial law.

The ceremonial law—regulations for religious worship concerning burnt offerings, sacrifices, and all other rituals or ceremonies connected with Israel's worship in the temple and elsewhere: Any careful study of the offerings, the sacrifices, and the typology will reveal that

- Christ is the sacrifice typified in the Old Testament ceremonial sacrifices.
- He is the offering.
- He is the altar.
- He is the High Priest.

He has not only shed His blood, but has also presented it in heaven. All the ceremonial law was fulfilled in Him (cf. Heb. 9–10).

The moral law—the Ten Commandments: Jesus obeyed the will of His Father in every respect. He kept the commandments. And He died for people who have not kept the commandments. That is what the cross and Christianity are all about.

Paul sums up the work of Christ this way: "Christ has redeemed us from the curse of the law, having become a curse for us (for it is written, 'Cursed is everyone who hangs on a tree'" (Gal. 3:13).

Other Senses in Which Jesus Fulfilled the Law

We noted earlier that Jesus fulfilled the law by restoring its proper use and meaning when He repeatedly challenged the Pharisees' teaching by His words "But *I* say." We have also seen how Jesus performed personal, perfect, perpetual obedience to the precepts of the law, and yet suffered its penalty upon the cross for His people—His active and passive obedience.

Some other senses of fulfillment of the law deserve mention. Jesus fulfills the law in reference to both believer and unbeliever. In believers' hearts He imparts faith so that they come to Him trusting in the One who alone fulfilled the law. His Spirit implants within them a love for the law and gives them the power and desire to keep it (Rom. 8:2-4; Jer. 31:33-34).

> To see the law by Christ fulfilled,
> And hear His pardoning voice,
> Changes a slave into a child,
> And duty into choice.

How does Christ fulfill the law in the unbeliever? He executes the curse of the law upon the reprobate. "Cursed is everyone who does not continue in all things which are written in the book of the law, to do them" (Gal. 3:10).

There is also a sense in which Jesus came to fulfill the law by completing the revelation. He holds Himself up as the One who "finished the work" (John 17:4). The writer of Hebrews explains, "God, who at various times and in different ways spoke in time past to the fathers by the prophets, has in these last days spoken to us by His Son" (Heb. 1:1-2).

A form of the word translated "fulfill" in Matthew 5:17 is used also in Romans 15:19, where Paul says, "I have fully preached the gospel of Christ." Just as Paul fully, clearly, and completely, unfolded the gospel of Christ, so our Lord fully, clearly, and completely fulfilled the law. In doing so, He corrected its wrong use, restored its spiritual meaning, and upheld it as God's eternal standard of righteousness.

CHAPTER TWELVE

The Law and Grace

*"Sin shall not have dominion over you, for you are
not under law but under grace." (Rom. 6:14)*

THE LAW WAS GIVEN that grace might be sought; grace was given
that the law might be fulfilled. To put it another way: Paul, as
a Pharisee, thought that people should keep the law in order to
be saved. As a Christian, he saw that people must be saved in
order that they might keep the law.

My purpose in this chapter is to show that a Christian is not
a lawless person and that there is a particular connection between the law and grace. To press moral duties without a
proper declaration of the grace of God in Christ Jesus is to deceive souls, leading them away from the biblical gospel and
their relationship with God's moral law. Grace alone enables us
to live up to those eternal standards, rendering our lives acceptable to God as we live in dependence on Him.

"Not Under Law"

One of the most misquoted, misunderstood, and misapplied
verses in all the Bible is Romans 6:14. The second part of the
verse is usually quoted out of context: "You are not under law
but under grace." Quoting only that part of the verse while ig-
noring the first clause ("Sin shall not have dominion over you")

distorts the meaning of the passage altogether. To do so is to separate what God has joined together, and the sad result of this separation is a generation of lost, lawless, antinomian church members.

Romans 6:14 has reference to justification, that is, our acceptance with God. Our hope of acceptance before God is not by keeping the law, but by the blood and righteousness of Christ, our Savior and Lord. The whole context of Romans 3-5 concerns justification. There is an antithesis between law and grace in respect to justification—we are justified by grace, not by law. But there is also a vital relationship between law and grace. "Do we then make void the law through faith? Certainly not! On the contrary, we establish the law" (Rom. 3:31). The law makes grace necessary by showing us that we are sinners: "By the law is the knowledge of sin" (3:20). Where there is no law, there is no transgression. It is by the power of grace that the law is established.

The Heidelberg Catechism is organized according to the three great themes: *guilt, grace, and gratitude* (cf. Q. 2). How do we know guilt? By the law—sin is the transgression of the law (1 John 3:4). How do we know grace? By the revelation of Christ to our hearts, that is, who He is, what He did, why He did it, where He is now, and His coming again. How do the recipients of grace express gratitude? (1) By loving obedience—"If you love Me, keep My commandments," said Jesus (John 14:15); (2) by loyal service—"Why do you call Me 'Lord, Lord,' and do not do the things which I say?" (Luke 6:46); (3) by a longing to be conformed to Christ, becoming like Jesus:

- in His love to do the Father's will—"Behold, I have come—in the volume of the book it is written of Me— to do Your will, O God" (Heb. 10:7).
- in His deep compassion for sinners—"the Son of Man has come to seek and to save that which was lost" (Luke 19:10).
- in His purity of heart—He was separate from sinners.
- in His true humility—He was humility personified.

The doctrine of grace must be jealously guarded against the distortion of justification by the works of the law. But it is equally important that the doctrine of the law be preserved against a wrong conception of its relationship to grace. The law has a proper function in the economy of grace. Therefore, we must not set up a false antithesis between law and grace by quoting a half verse ("You are not under law but under grace") so as to imply that the Christian has nothing to do with the Ten Commandments.

No Dominion

Romans 6:14 makes a declaration: "Sin shall not have dominion over you." This is not an exhortation, but rather a statement of fact. The reason it is true is that you are under grace. The law has no dominion over the Christian. Why? Because of the mighty power of grace. The law has dominion over every unconverted person because he is under the dominion of sin, and to be under the dominion of sin is to be under the dominion of the law. The law has no power to save or sanctify, but it does have power to condemn and damn. Every creature, by virtue of his creaturehood, is either under the dominion of the Creator's law or under the dominion of grace, which is the dominion of Christ.

I am not suggesting that the Christian is without sin. Sin is still in the Christian and often has great power to hinder him from doing good. Sin still entices and ensnares. It may bring the Christian into captivity and may seem at times to reign. But the assurance of this verse is what it says cannot be: "Sin shall not have dominion over you." If you are born again, sin is dethroned, you are born into another kingdom, and you have another King— King Jesus. The kingdom of Christ is the kingdom of grace.

Romans 6:14 offers great assurance of final preservation by the Savior. Sin shall not have dominion over you, Christian! That is encouragement, hope, and assurance.

In addition to this assurance of being granted grace, there is stability in knowing that the standards do not change. Grace never changes what is right, and *the moral law is right*. Grace gives us power to do right. It does not set up some new standard of right. Grace is, therefore, vitally related to that one eternal standard of righteousness summarized in the Ten Commandments. In that relationship, there are some things that this eternal standard *can do,* and there are some things that it *cannot do.*

What the Law Can Do

- The law commands and demands. It sets before all people the will of God, the only true objective standard of moral righteousness.
- The law pronounces the judgment of condemnation upon every lawbreaker (just as in our civil laws, if a man robs a bank, the judgment of the court is upon him because he is a lawbreaker). The law has nothing but a curse for lawbreakers. "Cursed is everyone who does not continue in all things which are written in the book of the law, to do them" (Gal. 3:10).
- The law exposes and convicts of sin. The law is spiritual (Rom. 7:14), and as the Word of God, it is living and powerful, searching the thoughts and intents of the heart. "What shall we say then? Is the law sin? Certainly not! On the contrary, I would not have known sin except through the law" (Rom. 7:7).

What the Law Cannot Do

- The law cannot justify the lawbreaker. Law as law has no provision to make us right with God. There is no forgiving grace in the law. It gives no power to fulfill its own demands.
- The law knows no clemency for the remission of guilt.
- The law provides no righteousness to meet our iniquity.
- The law exerts no constraining power to restore or reclaim our waywardness.
- The law knows no mercy to melt our hearts in penitence and new obedience.

God views us through the lens of either the law or grace, and no one can be under both at once, as far as justification is concerned. The law has no strength to dethrone sin or to destroy sin. It discovers sin and condemns sin, but gives no strength to oppose it. The law directs us to the right road to travel but gives no strength for the journey.

> *Run and work, the law demands*
> *But gives me neither feet nor hands.*
> *A sweeter sound the gospel brings,*
> *It bids me fly and gives me wings.*

Though the law is just, it cannot justify sinners. Though the law is good, it cannot make sinners good or deliver them from the power of sin. Though the law is holy, it cannot make sinners holy who have made themselves unholy. Our text, Romans 6:14, teaches us that the law can do nothing to relieve the bondage or dominion of sin. It is in this light that we have the apostle's wonderful expression "not under law but under grace."

Oh! That wonderful word, "grace." "Grace, grace—marvelous grace." "Amazing grace—how sweet the sound!" Grace is the sovereign will and power of God, not for regulating thought and conduct but for delivering people from the thought and conduct that binds them as slaves to unholiness.

Grace is the deliverance from the dominion of sin (which is the transgression of the law). Yes, there is an antithesis in respect to justification between the function and power of the law, on the one hand, and the function and power of grace, on the other. But, this antithesis does not mean that all relevance of the law to the believer is abolished in Romans 6:14.

Not Lawless

My main point is to show that the Christian is not lawless or without a standard of righteousness. I could show this from many passages, but I will focus on just one passage, 1 Corinthians 9:20-21 (and compare it with Rom. 6:14): "To the Jews I became as a Jew, that I might win Jews; to those who are under the law, as under the law, that I might win those are under the law; to those who are without law, as without law (*not being without law toward God, but under the law toward Christ*), that I might win those who are without law."

Paul is saying that he is not lawless in respect to God; he is law-bound in respect to Christ. The expression "under law to Christ" means "bound in the law to Christ, or under the obligation of the law of Christ." First Corinthians 9:20-21 does not contrast the law of God and the law of Christ. Paul does not say, "I am not *under* the law of God but under the law of Christ," Rather, he says "not being *without* law toward God." The implication is that he *is* under law to God, and this "under law toward God" finds its validation and explanation in his being under law toward Christ.

Clearly Paul was "not without law to God" *because* he was "under the law to Christ." God the Father and God the Son do not have two different standards of righteousness for creatures or new creatures—that would mean conflict in the Trinity. This passage teaches us that Christ gave commandments in harmony with the Ten Commandments (see also Matt. 5:17-48). Here is the same law that Moses gave in Exodus 20:1–17. Therefore, Romans 6:14 cannot mean we are not under law in any sense, cut off from *any* fixed objective standard of conduct. To take half of this verse and set up a false antithesis between law and grace, one misses the whole teaching of this wonderful verse. This verse is meant for assurance that sin shall not have dominion over those who are under grace. To be under grace is to have a saving interest in the gospel, with all the rights, privileges, and benefits of the gospel.

> *The terrors of law and of God*
> *With me can have nothing to do;*
> *My Savior's obedience and blood*
> *Hide all my transgressions from view.*

A most important word in this verse is *"dominion."* Sin has dominion over people in their unregenerate state. After con-

version, sin is still in the Christian and often has great power
to hinder good or to promote evil. Sin still entices, ensnares, and
brings the Christian into captivity, seeming as though it might
reign again. But our verse assures us that *it will not have dominion.* Why? Because the Christian is under the power and dominion of grace! "Bless the Lord, O my soul" (Ps. 103:1).

Romans 6:14 is expressing more than what *ought not* to be; it
tells us what *cannot* be and *shall not* be. It is an absolute promise:
Sin shall not have dominion over true believers. It is speaking
of sin's tyrannical, governing power. It shall not "lord it over
you," Christian! In regeneration, sin is dethroned. Christ enters
as Lord and continues to be so. Saints are of another kingdom—
the kingdom of Christ, the kingdom of grace. If sin could reign
over Christians, they could be lost and perish. But this can
never be!

The supposed proof-text for antinomianism turns out to be
a few words in a verse that tells us why sin shall not have dominion over us—because we are not under law but under
grace. This verse does not set up an antithesis between law and
grace. It teaches us why the recipients of grace will not be lawless. The antinomians undermine the Ten Commandments on
the basis of half a verse—and that robbed of its true meaning!

No exposition of any text is right that does not agree with the
principles of Christianity set down in the Apostle's Creed, the
Lord's Prayer, and the Ten Commandments. When you have
only one passage of Scripture on which to form an important
doctrine, on closer examination you will probably find you
have no basis for that belief.

The Context of Romans 6:14

Let us consider the broader context of Romans 6:14, the sur-
rounding chapters in the book of Romans. As mentioned earlier, the apostle in Romans 3-5 is talking about *justification:* "If
Abraham was *justified* by works, he has something of which to
boast, but not before God" (4: 2); "[Jesus] was delivered up because of our offenses, and was raised because of our *justifica-*

tion" (4: 25); "Therefore, having been *justified* by faith, we have peace with God through our Lord Jesus Christ" (5:1).

Justification by faith alone presented two problems among the Jews. The first problem was the idea that the more we sin, the more we experience grace. Paul wrote in Romans 5:20-21, "The law entered that the offense might abound. But where sin abounded, grace abounded much more, so that as sin reigned in death, even so grace might reign through righteousness to eternal life through Jesus Christ our Lord." But Paul anticipates how his readers might well misuse that truth: "What shall we say then? Shall we continue in sin that grace may abound? Certainly not! How shall we who died to sin live any longer in it?" (Rom. 6:1). And so, chapter 6 continues the discussion of justification, but now in terms of our need for sanctification.

The second problem for the Jews is their suspicion that Paul was doing away with the law. Paul addresses this in Romans 7, the best chapter to show the believer's relationship to the law.

When Paul states in Romans 6:14 that sin shall not lord it over believers, he offers a glorious promise of encouragement. Let us examine this verse more closely.

Two "For's" in Romans 6:14

The little word "for" at the beginning of verse 14 is extremely important. It connects verse 14 to the immediate context, verses 12–13, which are part of a complete statement. Therefore, verses 12–14 should be considered together.

I have stressed that verse 14 is not a command or an exhortation, but a statement of fact, a statement of promise, encouragement, and assurance. It explains verses 12–13, giving reason why we should and can obey the commands in those two verses. Why should you "not let sin reign in your mortal body" (v. 12) and "not present your members as instruments of unrighteousness" (v. 13)? *"For* [because] sin shall not have dominion over you."

There is a second "for" in verse 14. Can you not picture someone saying to the apostle Paul, "How can you make such a

dogmatic statement—"Sin shall not have dominion over you"?
He answers, *"For* you are not under law but under grace." This
explains the first statement and why the first statement can be
made so confidently.

To what law is the apostle referring here? Not all expositors
agree. I am of the opinion (and I am in good company) that Paul
refers not only to the Mosaic law here but also to law in general, that is, the law as a principle binding on every creature
apart from Christ. Earlier Paul wrote that "when Gentiles, who
do not have the law, by nature do the things contained in the
law, these, although not having the law, are a law to themselves, who show the work of the law written in their hearts,
their conscience also bearing witness, and between themselves
their thoughts accusing or else excusing them" (Rom. 2:14–15).
In other words, the non-Christian is under law by the fact that
he is a creature upon whose heart the law was written. Therefore, the Gentiles who never heard of the law of Moses were
under law, for they were a law unto themselves. By the law
written on their hearts they were able to accuse or excuse one
another. The whole of mankind is under a principle of law.

Being under law means that you have to justify yourself in
the presence of God by your own actions, works, and deeds.
Law as a means of justification comes to man and says, "Do this
and you shall live," meaning not at all what Moses and Christ
meant by that phrase—do this in humble faith and live. Being
under the law apart from true faith in the Redeemer is nothing
more than self-righteousness.

Why is the apostle so concerned to say that we are not under
law? Because it is the only way we can understand the truth he
has already stated, namely, that "sin shall not have dominion
over you." That question is more fully answered in Romans 7-
8:4. There Paul shows us exactly what Romans 6:14 means. His
position is that no law of any kind can deliver us from the
power of sin.

In an earlier chapter, I pointed out that one of the difficulties
of dealing with the law is the many ways in which the word is
used in the Bible. Sometimes *law* is used as a principle, as in Ro-

mans 7:21–23 and 8:2. Sin remains a law, a principle, in Christians, but not a law that has complete dominion over them, as over unbelievers. "The law of the Spirit of life in Christ Jesus has made me free from the law of sin and death" (Rom. 8:2). In the believer this sin principle exerts force but has lost its ultimate power to rule.

Laws are accompanied by rewards and punishments. The reward of sin is its temporary gratification, "the passing pleasures of sin" (Heb. 11:25). By this sorry reward the law of sin keeps the world in obedience to its commands, showing us what power it has to influence the minds of men. The pleasure of sin is the object that most people lose their souls to obtain.

But in Romans 6:14, Paul describes those who are no longer dominated by sin because they are no longer under the law of sin. And that raises some personal questions.

Romans 6:14 and You

Does this verse describe your life? Are you living under the law of sin, or have you been delivered from sin's dominion? What hope do you have for victory in your daily battle with your own sin? To answer those questions, Romans 6:14 offers first a test, then a promise, and finally an encouragement and assurance.

A Test

Does sin have dominion over you? Notice, I did not ask, Do you sin? "If we say that we have no sin, we deceive ourselves, and the truth is not in us. . . . If we say that we have not sinned, we make Him a liar, and His word is not in us" (1 John 1:8, 10). The question is not whether you obey perfectly but whether you manifest a genuine desire to obey as one set free from sin's dominion.

To expect the favor of the Lord without a habitual desire to conform to His image is one of the many delusions of a self-deceived soul. A Christian has an earnest desire to be delivered from the power of sin as much as he desires to be delivered from the guilt and penalty of sin. The true Christian has prayed for acceptance. Now, as a Christian, he cries for holiness: "Let no iniquity have dominion over me" (Ps. 119:133).

The throne of our hearts allows only one ruler. Therefore, although grace and sin may and do co-exist within, they *cannot* be partners on the throne. Thus David prayed in Psalm 19:13, "Keep back Your servant also from presumptuous sins; let them not have dominion over me. Then I shall be blameless, and I shall be innocent of great transgression."

Sin, even when subdued, will struggle to the last to have dominion. But by looking to Jesus, we will have the victory (Rom. 7:25; 8:1.) The clearer our view of Jesus, the more complete will be our victory. "And this is the victory that has overcome the world—our faith" (1 John 5:4). He continually gives us strength so that sin cannot have dominion.

A Promise

Romans 6:14 promises that "sin shall not *have dominion over* you," not that sin shall not *dwell in* you. In the holiest Christian, there is enough remaining sin to destroy him if it were not for the grace of God, which restrains its deadly operation. Alas, some of God's choicest saints have fallen: David, Peter, and many since. The promise is in the words "dominion" and "grace."

"Sin shall not have dominion over you." A sheep may stumble into a ditch, but it will not be at home in the mud. If a hog falls into the muddy ditch, however, it will be fully at home and wallow in it.

Notice, the reason attached to the promise. Why won't sin have dominion over you? You are under the power of grace. There is no power in the law to save, to sanctify, or to preserve you. The power is in grace. Sin shall not have dominion, because, though sin is strong, grace is stronger. Satan is strong but grace is stronger. There will be awful wars within you because of remaining sin. *But*—another wonderful word in the Bible— sin shall not have dominion over you.

Yes, Christian, you sin, but you have not signed a peace treaty with sin. True, you are not perfectly holy, but you would like to be. The bent and bias of your mind is toward righteousness if you are a Christian indeed. And with Paul you can be "confident of this very thing, that He who has begun a good work in you will complete it until the day of Jesus Christ" (Phil. 1:6).

Encouragement and Assurance

This verse offers great encouragement and assurance to believers in various stages of their struggle with sin. Some Christians are very weak. If you are a weak Christian, you should find encouragement in the truth that sin shall no more have dominion over the weak or over the strong. Some of you are fighting with great sins. But if you are a real Christian, your battle with sin is not in vain. Sin shall not have dominion. You are not under law but under grace, and there is power in grace. You may be a young Christian still in the early stages of warfare with your past habits. Sin shall not have dominion over you; you are under grace. You may be a backslider—you have fallen back into sin. You will be chastened, but sin shall not have dominion over you.

There are two principles in the world that are meant to promote holiness. The one is the principle of *law* and *duty,* and the other is the principle of *grace* and *faith.*

Yes, Christian, there is a law of sin remaining—that is why you have an inward warfare (Rom. 7:23.) But there is also grace. John Newton phrased it beautifully in a hymn.

THE INWARD WARFARE
Galatians 5:17

Strange and mysterious is my life,
What opposites I feel within!
A stable peace, a constant strife;
The rule of grace, the power of sin:
Too often I am captive led,
Yet daily triumph in my Head.
I prize the privilege of prayer,
But oh! what backwardness to pray!

Though on the Lord I cast my care,
I feel its burden every day;
I seek his will in all I do,
Yet find my own is working too.
I call the promises my own,
And prize them more than mines of gold.
Yet though their sweetness I have known,
They leave me unimpressed and cold:
One hour upon the truth I feed,
The next I knew not what I read.
I love the holy day of rest,
When Jesus meets his gathered saints:
Sweet day, of all the week the best!
For its return my spirit pants;
Yet often, through my unbelief
It proves a day of guilt and grief.
While on my Savior I rely,
I know my foes shall love their aim,
And therefore dare their power defy,
Assured of conquest through his name;
But soon my confidence is slain,
And all my fears return again.
Thus different powers within me strive,
And grace and sin by turns prevail;
I grieve, rejoice, decline, revive,
And victory hangs in doubtful scale:
But Jesus has his promise past,
That grace shall overcome at last.

Sin, the Perplexing Indweller

Sin is always ready to apply itself to every end and purpose. That is what caused the apostle Paul to say that *when he would do good*, evil was present with him. If you want to pray, if you wish to hear the Word of God, to give, to meditate, to work righteousness, to resist temptation—you can be sure this troublesome, perplexing indweller will be present with you. As you try to apply your mind to anything good, there it is, in ignorance, darkness, vanity, folly, and madness. If you would engage your will to some good end, there it is also in spiritual deadness, stubbornness, and the roots of obstinacy—the ever-present indweller. Are your heart and affections set on some good work? This indwelling sin is present.

Do you find this principle in you? What experience do you have with its power? Is it always putting forth its poison in all your duties when you would do good? Oh! our need for spiritual wisdom, for supplies of grace, and assistance of the Holy Spirit!

My dear readers, I may not have fully explained this wonderful verse, but I do not want you to miss three things:

- The safe and peculiar position of the true believer: not under law but under grace.
- The special assurance given to the true believer: "Sin shall not have dominion over you."
- The remarkable reason given as to why sin shall not have dominion over you: "for you are not under law but under grace."

Well did Philip Doddridge speak of this marvelous grace in his hymn:

> *Grace! 'tis a charming sound,*
> *Harmonious to mine ear;*
> *Heaven with the echo shall resound,*
> *And all the earth shall hear.*
> *Grace first contrived a way*
> *To save rebellious man,*
> *And all the steps that grace display*
> *Which drew the wondrous plan.*
> *Grace taught my wand'ring feet*
> *To tread the heavenly road*
> *And new supplies each hour I meet*
> *While pressing on to God.*
> *Grace all the work shall crown*

Through everlasting days;
It lays in heaven the top most stone
And well deserves the praise. Amen.

ROMANS 6:14, "You are not under law but under grace," does not set up an antithesis between law and grace. The biblical message is not law *or* grace, but law *and* grace.

It bears repeating that what God has joined together, no man should put asunder. And He has joined His love and His law. He has joined His grace and His law. The law was given that grace might be sought; grace was given that the law might be fulfilled.

CHAPTER THIRTEEN

The Relationship of the Law, Moses, and Christ (1)

*"The law was given through Moses, but grace and truth
came through Jesus Christ." (John 1:17)*

THE RELATIONSHIP OF THE LAW, MOSES, AND CHRIST has everything to do with the relationship between the Old and New Testaments. Erroneous views about the one relationship will produce problems in one's understanding of the other. Therefore, it is important that we first look at the relationship between the Testaments.

The law and the gospel encompass the whole Bible, but not as separate parts of the Bible. It is not as though some books of Scripture are exclusively law and others are gospel, or that the Old Testament is law only and the New is gospel. The law and the gospel are declared in each of them. In the Old Testament we find much of the gospel, and in the New Testament we find much of the law. Where the blessings of salvation are declared, offered, and promised freely—not conditioned on works performed by sinners—all such passages, whether in the Old Testament or in the New, contain the doctrine of the gospel.

Does Galatians Nullify the Old Testament?
Marcion's Division
The erroneous division of the Testaments is not new. In the early church, a religious teacher by the name of Marcion drove

a wedge between the Old and New Testaments. A native of Pontus (Sinope) who made his way to Rome about the year A.D. 139, Marcion is said to have been a man of deep earnestness and marked ability. Having labored unsuccessfully to bring the church to his way of thinking, he felt constrained to organize his followers into a separate church and to seek universal acceptance of his views by active propaganda.

Marcion thought that the book of Galatians held the key to the relationship between the Old Testament and the New. Noting that Galatians speaks of Judaistic opposition to Paul, Marcion proceeded on the assumption that the other apostles shared in this opposition. He became convinced that the gospel was corrupted by any mixture with the law. So he set himself to the task of separating the law and the gospel, and worked out his own theory of opposites or antitheses. Believing that Paul was the only apostle who really understood the gospel of Jesus Christ, Marcion limited the canon of the New Testament to the gospel of Luke and ten Epistles of Paul.

Marcion's basic error was twofold. First, he did not properly interpret the book of Galatians. Second, he based his view of the law on Galatians alone. Most antinomians are guilty of the same basic error. Interpretation of any single passage of Scripture requires our use of "the analogy of Scripture" (comparing Scripture with Scripture) as a rule of interpretation.

Comparing Galatians with Romans

The book of Galatians is dealing with a specific problem. The misguided Judaizers wanted to combine the gospel of Christ with the observance of Jewish ceremonies—a practice that had been rejected at the so-called apostolic council at Jerusalem (Acts 15:1ff.). Note that the problem addressed at the council was mixing Jewish *ceremonies* and the gospel, not mixing *the moral law* with the gospel. The Jerusalem council was about circumcision, not the Ten Commandments.

> And certain men came down from Judea and taught the brethren, "Unless you are circumcised according to the

custom of Moses, you cannot be saved." Therefore, when Paul and Barnabas had no small dissension and dispute with them, they determined that Paul and Barnabas and certain others of them should go up to Jerusalem, to the apostles and elders, about this question. (Acts 15:1–2)

"The question" here was circumcision.

We saw in the previous chapter that in his letter to the Romans, Paul upheld the role of the law in the believer's life, particularly in Romans 7. Paul did not change his mind or contradict himself concerning the role of the moral law between his writing to the Romans and his writing to the Galatians. First, in writing to the Galatians, he makes it very plain that the law is of divine origin (Gal. 3:19), that it is also an evidence of God's grace (v. 21), and that, despite all its severity, it was intended to make room for Christ (v. 23ff.). Such considerations serve to magnify the importance and the holy character of the law.

Second, it must be remembered that in Galatians (unlike Romans) the whole argument is governed by Paul's dispute with the Judaizers, who after the advent of Christ, wanted to bind believers to the ceremonies of Moses (the ceremonial law). It is altogether natural, therefore, that in such a discussion, the provisional and negative significance of the law should receive emphasis. In Romans, meanwhile, the argument is more balanced. It slants less toward the dangers of keeping the law and is oriented more toward its positive and permanent significance.

We can therefore say that Galatians emphasized the *inadequacy of the law for salvation*, and Romans emphasized that *despite the transgression of God's holy law, there is salvation in Christ*.

Almost every honest Bible teacher would agree that *most* of Paul's references to "law" in Galatians pertain to ceremonies, particularly circumcision (2:3, 7-9, 12; 5:2–12; 6:11–15; cf. Acts 15:1ff.). All would agree that the main theme of Galatians is the gospel of justification by faith apart from works of the law. No one was ever justified before God by the law. No law was ever given that could impart life. The law served only in a preparatory way—as a custodian bringing sinners to Christ to be justified freely. But there is more to salvation than justification. There are sanctification and glorification, and they are inseparably joined together in God's salvation. The epistle to the Romans also deals with justification, but not apart from sanctification.

A key phrase in Galatians 4:9–10 illustrates what I am saying: "But now after you have known God, or rather are known by God, how is it that you turn again to the weak and beggarly elements, to which you desire again to be in bondage? You observe days and months and seasons and years." Paul is here referring to that which kept his readers in bondage, who were seeking to be justified by ceremonies: "weak and beggarly elements." The New International Version says, "weak and miserable principles," namely, legalistic stipulations, ceremonies such as circumcision. In light of the positive things Paul says in Romans about the moral law, he must be referring in Galatians to ceremony, not morality. Otherwise, those two letters would be in blatant contradiction, and the Bible does not contradict itself.

The law to which Paul refers in Romans hardly sounds like "weak and miserable principles." Listen to the inspired words of the apostle: "By the law is the knowledge of sin" (Rom. 3:20). "Do we then make void the law through faith? On the contrary, we establish the law" (v. 31). Does that suggest that the moral law was weak? Far from it. Paul attributes his conversion to the law—the tenth commandment (Rom. 7:7-9). Though the law is weak and poor to save (just as the sinner is weak and poor), the law has the power to convict. Not only is it powerful, but it is also holy, just, and good (vv. 12, 16). Paul must be talking about the Ten Commandments, not the ceremonial law. Surely he would not call something that is weak, beggarly, and miserable "good"! Nor would he say "I delight in the law of God" (v. 22) if he were referring to weak and miserable principles (the ceremonies) that have passed away.

Thus, while Paul emphasizes the passing of the ceremonial law in Galatians, that is not all that he has to say about law. In Romans he emphasizes the abiding goodness, relevance, and authority of the moral law. The two letters must be understood together, for they mutually serve each other. We must not take our view of the law from the book of Galatians *alone*.

Paul's focus on circumcision in Galatians is plain in 5:2–12. Likewise, his personal benediction near the end of the letter (6:11–15) reinforces the principal concern of his letter, that justification is through the cross, not through circumcision or other legalistic stipulations.

> See with what large letters I have written to you with my own hand! As many as desire to make a good showing in the flesh, these try to compel you to be circumcised, only that they may not suffer persecution for the cross of Christ. For not even those who are circumcised keep the law, but they desire to have you circumcised that they may glory in your flesh. But God forbid that I should glory except in the cross of our Lord Jesus Christ, by whom the world has been crucified to me, and I to the world. For in Christ Jesus neither circumcision nor uncircumcision avails anything, but a new creation.

It should not go unnoticed that between these two passages in Galatians, Paul upholds the moral law by calling his readers to "walk in the Spirit" (5:16) and "not use liberty as an opportunity for the flesh." And what does the Spirit teach us to do? To fulfill the righteous principles of the law in our walk: "that the righteous requirement of the law might be fulfilled in us who do not walk according to the flesh but according to the Spirit" (Rom. 8:4).

Therefore, the book of Galatians should not be used to drive a wedge between the moral law and the gospel, or between the Old Testament and the New. The book of Galatians must be interpreted in the light of the whole Bible. Having said that, we can now look at the real similarities and differences between the Testaments and between Moses and Christ.

Similarities and Differences

There are many such similarities and differences between the Old and New Testaments. For a good exposition of them, I suggest reading John Calvin, *The Institutes of the Christian Religion*, 2.10–11.

Basic Similarities

The similarities may be summarized this way: All the people of God from the beginning of time have been adopted into His family and covenanted to Him by the same law, the same doctrines, and the same grace. They participate in the same inheritance and enjoy the same salvation by grace through the same Mediator. *The people of God have never been saved any other way than by grace.*

They had the same faith in the same Mediator (yet to come) as did the saints of the New Testament. We read about their faith in Hebrews 11. Paul confirms this in Romans 1:2-3 when he writes of the gospel "which He promised before through His prophets in the Holy Scriptures, concerning His Son Jesus Christ our Lord, who was born of the seed of David according to the flesh."

Paul is saying that the righteousness of God apart from the law is revealed through the law and the prophets. Jesus likewise speaks of the revelation of His gospel to Old Testament saints: "Your father Abraham rejoiced to see My day, and he saw it and was glad" (John 8:56).

Mary and Zacharias, in their songs about the coming of Jesus, confirmed the hope of the Old Testament people of God in the gospel: "He has helped His servant Israel, in remembrance of His mercy, as He spoke to our fathers, to Abraham and to his seed forever" (Luke 1:54-55). "Blessed is the Lord God of Israel, for He has visited and redeemed His people . . . to perform the mercy promised to our fathers and to remember His holy covenant, the oath which He swore to our father Abraham" (vv. 68, 72-73).

Moses Versus Jesus in John 1:17?

We saw in chapter 12 how Romans 6:14 is mistaken to mean that Christians are not under the law in any sense. Another verse that is badly misinterpreted and misapplied is John 1:17. "For the law was given through Moses, but grace and truth came through Jesus Christ."

We must remember that Moses was not the lawgiver. He was the messenger, the deliverer. There is only one Lawgiver, God almighty, our Creator. It was He who wrote the Ten Commandments on tables of stone. And so, to be exact, they are not the law of *Moses;* they are the law of *God.* Christ, the Mediator of the new covenant, is not a new Lawgiver. It was His eternal law that was revealed to Moses in the first place. He need not improve upon it or replace it.

Often Bible teachers see a radical opposition between Moses and Jesus in John 1:17. That is a great error and does much harm. Moses and Christ are friends. It is impossible to tarnish the glory of the one without dulling the luster of the other. Jesus therefore said to Jews who wished to kill Him, "If you believed Moses, you would believe Me; for he wrote about Me. But if you do not believe his writings, how will you believe My words?" (John 5:46-47). Later He said to the disciples on the road to Emmaus, "These are the words which I spoke to you while I was still with you, that all things must be fulfilled which were written in the Law of Moses and the Prophets and the Psalms concerning Me" (Luke 24:44).

To be sure, there are important differences between Moses and Christ—day-and-night differences. *But* there is also a connection and a relationship. One of the fundamental principles in any consideration of the law and grace is that we must not miss that connection. And so these three facts should be fixed in our minds:

1. There is a vast difference between law and grace, Moses and Christ. The law came by Moses. Christ did not come down from Mount Sinai with the Ten Commandments. And Moses did not go to the cross. Grace and truth came by Jesus Christ.
2. There is also a vital, inseparable, immutable, and eternal connection between Moses and Christ. It is a major

error to overemphasize the difference without estab-
lishing the relationship.

3. Law and grace serve to establish each other. The law is
   the foundation, and grace and truth are the fulfillment.
   Together they form one glorious trinity: judgment,
   mercy, truth.

Moses and the law show men their disease and thus make
way for the Great Physician. (The healthy do not need a physician.) The law shows the need, thus it is the foundation.

Why do people get physical examinations? To discover any
hidden problems. And if a problem is discovered, they call for
the surgeon or the internist. The discovery of the disease and
the physician to heal—they are different but related. Both are
needed. The law threatens but cannot help, wounds but does
not heal, shows our feebleness but does not give strength. But
it does make us ready for the Great Physician, who brings heal-
ing and strength.

BELOW, I WISH TO DO THREE THINGS: First, I want to show what
John 1:17 is *not* teaching. Second, I want to make some key
comparisons between Moses and Christ. Third, I hope to draw
some reasonable conclusions concerning the contrast and connection between law and grace, between Moses and Christ.

What John 1:17 Does Not Teach

"The law was given through Moses, but grace and truth came
through Jesus Christ." What this verse does not teach is that
Moses was not a messenger of truth, or that the law he delivered was not true. Moses taught truth. The law was truth and
nothing but truth—no less true than Christ. He personified it.
The law was perfect and Christ was perfect.

The verse does not teach that Moses was false and Christ was
true. Though Moses was not perfect, he was a true servant of
God.

By faith Moses, when he became of age, refused to be called the son of Pharaoh's daughter, choosing rather to suffer affliction with the people of God than to enjoy the passing pleasures of sin, esteeming the reproach of Christ greater riches than the treasures in Egypt; for he looked to the reward. By faith he forsook Egypt, not fearing the wrath of the king; for he endured as seeing Him who is invisible. By faith he kept the Passover and the sprinkling of blood, lest he who destroyed the first-born should touch them. (Heb. 11:24-28)

Nor does the verse teach that Moses did not know anything about grace and a gracious God.

And the LORD passed before him and proclaimed, "The LORD, the LORD God, merciful and gracious, long-suffering, and abounding in goodness and truth, keeping mercy for thousands, forgiving iniquity and trans-gression and sin, by no means clearing the guilty, visiting the iniquity of the fathers upon the children and the children's children to the third and the fourth generation." So Moses made haste and bowed his head toward the earth, and worshiped. Then he said, "If now I have found *grace* in Your sight, O LORD, let my LORD, I pray, go among us, even though we are a stiff-necked people; and pardon our iniquity and our sin, and take us as Your inheritance." (Ex. 34:6-9)

Though grace and truth came through Jesus, they did not have to wait until His coming to earth. The grace of our Lord came as early as the fall of Adam and Eve. It was grace that sought them in the garden when they hid from God (Gen. 3:8). It was by grace that God called to them (v. 9). Truth sent the righteous judgment that expelled them from the garden (vv. 22-24), but mercy and grace provided for them (see, e.g., 3:15; 4:1, 25). Later we read that "Noah found grace in the eyes of the LORD" (Gen. 6:8).

God also dealt according to grace and truth with His people on the night of the Passover in Egypt. Grace provided their safety under the blood. And truth demanded an innocent substitute to atone for sin. These great events pictured the grace and truth that would come in Christ. Thus, John 1:17 must not be thought to teach that Moses knew nothing of grace. Nor does the passage teach that there is no relationship between law and grace.

In summary, John 1:17 cannot mean the following:

- It cannot mean that Moses did not teach truth; the law was truth.
- It cannot mean that Moses was false and Christ was true.
- It cannot mean that Moses did not know anything about grace.
- It cannot mean that there is any conflict between Moses and Christ, or between law and grace.
- It cannot mean that there is no relationship between law and grace or between Moses and Christ.

In the light of these five things that the passage cannot mean, there are some important conclusions that should be drawn.

- It is important to understand the relationship.
- It is important to see how Moses serves Christ to establish Him and His work on the cross (see "Fulfill" in chap. 11).
- It is important to see how the law serves to establish the gospel.
- It is important in teaching or preaching never to suggest any idea of opposition or contradiction between law and gospel or between Christ and Moses—not by interpretation, implication, illustration, or application.

There is *absolutely no opposition*. It is a serious, harmful error to say that there is. To oppose the law is also to oppose the life and death of the Savior. By the law, He fulfilled all righteousness and by His life and death He endured sin's penalty. By doing both He declared the law to be holy, just, and good. Every reflection, therefore, upon the moral law is a reflection upon Christ.

Comparisons Between Moses and Christ

Although John 1:17 does not envision a conflict between Moses and Christ, it invites a number of key comparisons.

- Moses was a servant. Christ was the Master.
- Moses was a subject. Christ was King of Kings and Lord of Lords.
- Moses was a man. Christ was the God-man.
- Moses was the agent smiting the rock. Christ was the smitten Rock.
- Moses was a student. Christ was the only divine teacher in whom dwelled the fullness of wisdom.
- Moses had a message of death to the sinner. Christ had the message of pardon, hope, and life.
- Moses was given the law. Christ was the essence of grace and truth. He was full of grace and truth (v. 14).
- Moses came from Mount Sinai with the law that condemned sinners. Christ went to Mount Calvary for condemned sinners.
- Moses did not see God. Christ was with God and was God (v. 1).

Conclusions Concerning Law and Grace

We may, therefore, draw some reasonable conclusions regarding the contrast and connection between law and grace.

- The law addressed men as members of the old creation. Grace makes men members of the new creation (2 Cor. 5:17).
- The law manifests the sin that is in man. Grace manifests the mercy that is in God.

- The law demands righteousness from man.
  Grace brings righteousness to man.
- The law sentences the living man to death.
  Grace brings dead men to life.
- The law speaks of what man must do for God.
  Grace tells what God has done for man.
- The law brings the knowledge of sin.
  Grace brings the remedy for sin.
- The law brings the will of God to man but gives no power to obey.
  Grace gives man a desire to do the will of God and gives him power to obey.
- The law testified to God's righteousness.
  Grace supplies and imparts His righteousness.

John 1:17 contrasts what was *given* by Moses and what *came* by Jesus Christ. Grace and truth were not merely given but came in all their fullness and glorious perfection in Christ. The law was given to Moses because it was not his own. But grace and truth were not given to Christ—they were His own essential perfections. The greatest comparison and contrast is how God was made known by *His only begotten Son*.

This wonderful verse is not describing a conflict between the Mosaic law and Christ. What we have in John 1:17 is a comparison. The saints under Moses were infants in knowledge, not having the full revelation of Christ in the New Testament. Those living in the New Testament age can see further now into the mystery of the gospel, understand it, and take great comfort in it.

Could those who separate Moses and Christ join in singing the song of Moses and the Lamb described in Revelation 15?

And they sing the song of Moses, the servant of God, and the song of the Lamb, saying: "Great and marvelous are Your works, Lord God Almighty! Just and true are Your ways, O King of the saints! Who shall not fear You, O Lord, and glorify Your name? For You alone are holy.

For all nations shall come and worship before You, For Your judgments have been manifested." (Rev. 15:3-4)

God's promises always accompany His precepts. His grace turns precepts into promises, and the spirit of grace turns precepts and promises into prayers. In this way, the law establishes grace and serves the gospel, rather than opposing it.

CHAPTER FOURTEEN

The Relationship of the Law, Moses, and Christ (2)

"If what was passing away was glorious, what remains is much more glorious." (2 Cor. 3:11)

SECOND CORINTHIANS 3 CONTRASTS the administration of the law and the administration of the gospel. It is another portion of Scripture that has been misinterpreted and misused by antinomians. There Paul makes several contrasts between, for example, the ministration of death and the ministration of Spirit or the ministration of the Spirit and the ministration of condemnation. He also contrasts glory with greater glory, the glorious with the much more glorious, the old covenant with the new covenant, that which was written on tablets of stone with that which was written on the heart, and the letter that kills with the Spirit that gives life. All these contrasts can be summed up in two words—*law* and *gospel*.

Patrick Fairbairn, D.D., in his valuable book, *The Revelation of Law in Scripture* (reprint, Phillipsburg, N.J.: Presbyterian and Reformed, 1996), said in reference to 2 Corinthians 3, "This is the most important passage on the law in St. Paul's epistles" (p. xii). It is important because it contrasts the glory of the old covenant with the greater glory of the new. Nowhere does this chapter say that there was no glory in the ministration of condemnation; in fact, it clearly says that the ministry of death was glorious (vv. 7, 9). The contrast is between the glory of the law and exceeding glory of the gospel (vv. 9, 11).

Philip E. Hughes, in his excellent commentary on 2 Corinthians, explained,

> The establishment of the new covenant, however, implies neither abrogation nor the depreciation of the Mosaic law. This is plainly shown by the terms in which God announces His new covenant: "I will put my law in their inward parts" (Jer. 31:33), and by the object it is intended to achieve: "that they may walk in my statutes, and keep mine ordinances, and do them" (Ezek. 11:20). There is not a question of a new law or of no law. Neither God changes nor His law. The difference between the old and the new covenants is that under the old that law is written on tablets of stone, confronting man as an external ordinance and condemning him because of his failure through sin to obey its commandments, whereas under the new the law is written internally within the redeemed heart by the dynamic regenerating work of the Holy Spirit, so that through faith in Christ, the only law keeper, and inward experience of His power man no longer hates but loves God's law, and is enabled to fulfil its precepts. Of course there were lovers of God's law in the Old Testament period; and it did not differ radically from New Testament believers. Their love had to be by divine grace granted to them. (*Paul's Second Epistle to the Corinthians* [Grand Rapids: Eerdmans, 1980], 96ff.)

Our Christian fathers have repeatedly emphasized that the Old Testament believers were men and women of faith in Christ. Their faith was in anticipation: "Your father Abraham rejoiced to see My day, and he saw it and was glad," Jesus said (John 8:56).

After naming many of the Old Testament saints, the author of Hebrews adds, "These all died in faith, not having received the promises, but having seen them afar off were assured of them" (Heb. 11:13).

We must also remember that the law is as vital a part of the new covenant as it was of the old covenant.

From Condemnation to Righteousness

One of the most striking comparisons of the law and gospel in Scripture appears in 2 Corinthians 3:9: "If the ministry of condemnation had glory, the ministry of righteousness exceeds much more in glory." Here the two ministries have their distinguishing epithets and exhibit their characteristic glory. A mind under the teachings of the Holy Spirit will discern a peculiar glory in both ministrations, and unless strangely warped by preconceived notions, will desire to retain the whole glory of both in the sense intended by their divine Author. It is impossible to have clear and consistent views of the plan of salvation without discerning the nature, spirituality, and unalterable authority of the divine law. An appreciation of that law will invariably bring the soul to admire and trust the free grace of the gospel. They are not at variance with each other, though some men would proclaim and perpetuate a war between them, while others would mingle and confound them, so that the glory of both is eclipsed.

The language of every Christian heart is, "I delight in the law of God according to the inner man" (Rom. 7:22). But this is language one can never use until, through the law, he is dead to the law. Then he rejoices that he is not under the law, but under grace, and proclaims in his whole life that he is not without law to God, but under the law to Christ. He knows that by the deeds of the law no flesh can be justified, and that justification is obtained by faith in the blood and righteousness of the Son of God. Yet he exclaims, "Do we then make void the law through faith? Certainly not! On the contrary, we establish the law" (Rom. 3:31). He joins Paul in the assertion that if righteousness comes by the law, then Christ is dead in vain. And with the apostle he unites in the desire that the righteousness of the law might be fulfilled in us, who walk not after the flesh, but after the Spirit. In short, Christ has delivered him from the curse of the law and made the law a blessing to him.

We never experience the preciousness of Christ until we have some knowledge of the sin that exists in our natures, exposing us to the curse and wrath of God. By the law is the knowledge of sin. Therefore the law, pointing out our need of Christ by condemning all our thoughts, words, and actions, endears Him to us as it leaves us no hope apart from Him. Its constant and perpetual demand is "Do this and live." And its awful threatening is "The soul that sins shall die." That demand and that threatening can never lose their authority or force.

Consequently, while the sinner is under the law, he remains under its curse, exposed to its threatening. And whenever this awful fact is discovered and felt, by the teachings of the Holy Spirit, the sinner instantly flees Mount Sinai and hastens to Calvary. He is unaware of his danger until he discerns the spirituality and extent of the law as it penetrates the conscience, reiterating its demands and refusing any abatement or compromise. Then he runs from the sin-avenging sword to touch the scepter of Jesus and receive pardon and life through Him.

The law ministers condemnation to the conscience every day—for every action, word, and thought—even in the most spiritual and holy of all the family of God as long as they are in this imperfect state. It can accept nothing but what is perfect, and herein appears its glory. For while it leaves us nothing in ourselves to boast of or trust in, it brings a large revenue of glory to Jesus, who is the end of the law for righteousness to every one who believes. The glorious suitableness of the gospel is never seen until the holy rigor of the law is felt. But when this schoolmaster enforces the task that we are utterly unable to perform and begins to afflict us with Sinai's terrors, at first we promise to do, and often set about doing, all that he requires. Then finding ourselves without strength or inclination to perform what is righteously enjoined of us, a surety or substitute becomes essential to our salvation. Then how precious does Jesus appear in this all-important character! And the Holy Spirit enables the soul to appropriate His perfect obedience and infinite merit, drives him to a new kind of obedience, and creates a love of the law, yes, a delight in it that he never before possessed.

It is not possible for any man to love the law until he sees it fulfilled by Christ; nor is it possible for that man to refrain from loving the law who feels a sweet assurance that he is delivered from its curse by the obedience and death of Christ. So then, the law revealing its purity, extent, and rigor, makes Christ precious to the soul, and the soul to whom Christ is precious must love the law as did David ("Oh, how I love Your law!"—Ps. 119:97) or Paul ("I delight in the law of God"—Rom. 7:22).

From Stony Tablets to Hearts of Flesh

In 2 Corinthians 3, we do see very clearly the superiority of the new covenant over the old, but this does not abrogate or set aside the Decalogue (the moral law). The new covenant transfers that law from the tables of stone to "tables of flesh, that is, of the heart" (v. 3), in fulfillment of Jeremiah's prophecy (Jer. 31:33). If, as seems likely, Paul's opponents in Corinth were Judaizers, who gloried in the law ("ministers of righteousness"— 2 Cor. 11:15), it is easy to see how the argument of this chapter would fall upon them with overwhelming force. Though the apostles did not support the Judaizers' teaching, their continued observance of the ceremonial law led the Judaizers to suppose that legalism was of the essence to their religion (cf. Galatians with the Jerusalem council of Acts 15).

What does 2 Corinthians 3:6 mean when it speaks of a "new covenant"? Defining *covenant* can be as difficult as providing an adequate definition of *mother*.

Some think that a covenant is an agreement between God and man—like a contract between two people. That is not quite accurate. The covenant offered by God to man was not a compact between two parties coming together on equal terms. The biblical use of *covenant* does involve the coming together of two parties—God and man—but the terms are appointed by God alone. It is not bilateral, as when a contractor sits down with an owner and both agree to do certain things. God's covenant is unilateral. He dictates the terms. He calls the shots.

The Old Testament scholar O. Palmer Robertson has defined a covenant as "a *bond in blood sovereignly administered.*" He explains, "When God enters into a covenantal relationship with men, he sovereignly institutes a life-and-death bond. A covenant is a bond in blood, or a bond of life and death, sovereignly administered" (*The Christ of the Covenants* [Phillipsburg, N.J.: Presbyterian and Reformed, 1980], 4).

Stated very simply, a covenant is a promise suspended upon a condition. The old covenant promised spiritual communion with God ("I will be your God, and you will be My people"). The precondition of that relationship was either perfect obedience (a condition that no fallen man could ever meet) or humble faith in a perfect substitute and dependence on God's mercy. What the old covenant could only foreshadow, the new covenant fully provides—that perfect, obedient substitute in Christ alone. Because God's covenant envisions a spiritual relationship, it calls for obedience from the heart, not merely outward acts or self-righteousness. Somehow the law had to get from external tablets of stone into spiritually transformed hearts. And that could only happen on the basis of the redemption accomplished by Christ and applied by His Spirit. The law without the Messiah could never produce genuine holiness, forgiveness, or communion with God.

Thus, the "new covenant" in 2 Corinthians 3 refers to the gospel of Christ as it surpasses the law yet to be fulfilled in Christ. To those who would use this passage to do away with the law, or to drive a wedge between the law and the gospel, it should be recalled that the law cannot be done away with. It is rewritten on the fleshly tables of the heart according to the promise in Jeremiah 31:33 quoted in Hebrews 10:16: "This is the covenant that I will make with them after those days, says the LORD: 'I will put My laws into their hearts, and in their minds I will write them.'" He does not say, "In the new covenant I will do away with the law." No, He says, "I will rewrite it." Second Corinthians 3 does not teach that the law was done away with.

How do we know? Because it was written on the heart, "not with ink but by the Spirit of the living God" (v. 3).

Some take 2 Corinthians 3 to mean that the law condemns and kills but the gospel does not condemn. But we learn from other parts of the Bible that the gospel does condemn and kill. Just a few verses earlier Paul wrote, "We [bearers of the gospel] are to God the fragrance of Christ among those who are being saved and among those who are perishing. To the one we are *the aroma of death to death,* and to the other the aroma of life to life. And who is sufficient for these things?" (2 Cor. 2:15–16).

Jesus said, "He who believes in Him is not condemned; but *he who does not believe is condemned already,* because he has not believed in the name of the only begotten Son of God" (John 3:18).

Devout old Simeon underscored this point (Luke 2:26-34). It had been revealed to him that he would not see death before he had seen the Lord's Christ (v. 26). Taking the baby Jesus in his arms (v. 28), he said, "This Child is destined for the fall and rising of many" (v. 34). Likewise, Peter spoke of Christ as "a stone of stumbling and a rock of offense" set for the ruin of many (1 Peter 2:8).

Paul describes gospel condemnation in the strongest terms.

> . . . when the Lord Jesus is revealed from heaven with His mighty angels, in flaming fire taking vengeance on those who do not know God, and on those who do not obey the gospel of our Lord Jesus Christ. These shall be punished with everlasting destruction from the presence of the Lord and from the glory of His power. (2 Thess. 1:7–9)

From Glory to Greater Glory

The royal, golden words "glory" and "glorious" appear ten times within five verses of 2 Corinthians 3 (7–11 NKJV). I have emphasized that Paul's contrast is not between that which had no glory and that which was glorious. The contrast is between glory and the more glorious. There was glory in the law (vv. 7, 9, 11). Paul calls the ministry of Moses a glorious ministry. No blame can be put on Moses for the divinely inspired truths he taught. In God's unfolding of revelation, Moses taught as much truth as the Israelites could bear. God used Moses to teach a high esteem for the law. The New Testament confirms this high regard for the law.

> Anyone who has rejected Moses' law dies without mercy on the testimony of two or three witnesses. Of how much worse punishment, do you suppose, will he be thought worthy who has trampled the Son of God underfoot, counted the blood of the covenant by which he was sanctified a common thing, and insulted the Spirit of grace? (Heb. 10:28-29)

Without denying that high view of the law, Paul in 2 Corinthians 3 exalts the glory of Christ and the gospel. Our Lord was glory personified. This world has never seen any glory comparable to that manifested in our blessed Savior.

What is glory, and what does it mean to be glorious? The glory of something is its true worth. To glorify something means to call attention to its value, to make much of it, to give it its due recognition. Glory includes such qualities as splendor, renown, and honor. When God is glorified in the true sense of the word, He is simply seen for who He is. His glory was often witnessed in the Old Testament, sometimes through some sort of physical manifestation.

But in the New Testament the glory of God is more fully personified. We learn that the Son is the radiance of God's glory and the exact representation of His nature: "[Jesus] being the brightness of [the Father's] glory and the express image of His person, and upholding all things by the word of His power, when He had by Himself purged our sins, sat down at the right hand of the Majesty on high" (Heb. 1:3).

Jesus thus exceeded the glory of the old covenant. The law was glorious. "But if the ministry of death, written and engraved on stones, was glorious . . . how will the ministry of the Spirit not be more glorious?" (2 Cor. 3:7-8). The apostle identified the ministry that brought death with letters engraved on stone (the Ten Commandments). If the divine origin of the old was authenticated by the radiance of Moses' face, how much more will the divine origin of the new be authenticated by transformed lives. The new ministry, which brings the Spirit of the living God to the hearts of men, is the ministry of life. The glory of the old enhances the greater glory of the new.

To understand glory we must study Christ. Where do you find the glory of God? "In the face of Jesus Christ" (2 Cor. 4:6). When do we see the glory of Christ?

1. When He spoke the glory shown through the veil of His flesh. No mere man ever spoke as He did. Some people saw it and were drawn to Him.
2. When He declared that He was the Redeemer, some people saw glory and believed.
3. When He said, "I am the resurrection," some people saw glory and believed Him and received hope.
4. When He acknowledged that He is God, some people saw glory in Him and believed. A man cannot speak that way about himself unless he is mentally ill or a lying blasphemer—or is telling the truth.
5. Some saw glory in His deeds. He spoke and the winds obeyed Him. He called men from the dead and there was power in His call to give life. Surely this was a display of His glory.
6. There was a glory about His death that caused fear to come to the hardest sinners. The centurion said, "Truly this was the Son of God!" (Matt. 27:54).
7. There was a glory about His death that caused the earth to shake and the veil in the temple to be torn, a glory about His death that caused graves to yield up their dead, and the sun to become black. What a display of glory!

Proclaiming the Surpassing Glory of Christ

I pray that God would raise up men who would know how to preach His glory, know how to preach Christ in such a way that men and women would see the glory of God in the face of Jesus Christ and be changed. Oh, that men and women could see the glory of His exaltation, His enthronement! They would fall on their faces as John did on the Isle of Patmos: "And when I saw Him, I fell at His feet as dead. But He laid His right hand on me, saying to me, 'Do not be afraid; I am the First and the Last. I am He who lives, and was dead, and behold, I am alive forevermore. Amen. And I have the keys of Hades and of Death'" (Rev. 1:17–18).

The only power that can change human lives and nations flows from the right hand of Him who sits on a throne. The reason the lives of lost church members are not changed is that they have never caught sight of the One who is on the throne. They have never seen the glory or felt the power of the One who could rightfully say, "All authority has been given to Me in heaven and on earth" (Matt. 28:18).

Stephen saw Him: "He, being full of the Holy Spirit, gazed into heaven and saw *the glory of God,* and Jesus standing at the right hand of God" (Acts 7:55).

Saul, going down the Road to Damascus, saw Him and was changed (Acts 9:3). He was blinded by a light from heaven—the glory of the Lord. There is glory around the throne. Some day this glory will be revealed again on this earth, and men will cry for the rocks and mountains to fall upon them (Rev. 6:12–17).

There is glory around the throne because that is where Jesus is. He came to that throne by way of His humble birth in a cow stable, and later through the depth of His humiliation on a bloody cross. But now He is exalted. "Therefore God also has highly exalted Him and given Him the name which is above every name, that at the name of Jesus every knee should bow, of those in heaven, and of those on earth, and of those under the earth, and that every tongue should confess that Jesus Christ is Lord, to the glory of God the Father" (Phil. 2:9–11).

The glory in the face of Jesus Christ far surpasses the glory in the face of Moses. "The ministry of death, written and engraved on stones, was glorious, so that the children of Israel could not look steadily at the face of Moses because of the glory of his countenance, which glory was passing away" (2 Cor 3:7). But the greatest glory—the glory connected with power—radiates in the face of God's Son: "For it is the God who commanded light to shine out of darkness who has shone in our hearts to give the light of the knowledge of the glory of God in the face of Jesus Christ" (2 Cor 4:6).

THERE IS A RELATIONSHIP between Moses and Christ, between law and grace. They are not in opposition or contradictory. The glory of the gospel exceeds but does not nullify the glory of the law. If you do not clearly understand the distinction, the connection, and the harmony between the law and grace, you will destroy the glory of both. Seeing how they serve each other will keep you from being entangled by the error of legalism, on the one hand, and of antinomianism, on the other. An understanding of the proper relationship between Moses and Christ will be a happy means of preserving your soul.

Never does Paul treat the old covenant in a disparaging manner by setting up an opposition. Quite the contrary, he attributes full honor to all of God's revelation. Paul does point out that the glory of the new covenant far exceeds the glory of the old. It is by comparison with the surpassing glory of the new covenant that the glory of the old may be said to have faded into insignificance (2 Cor. 3:10).

CHAPTER FIFTEEN

The Right and Wrong Uses of the Law

*"We know that the law is good if one
uses it lawfully." (1 Tim. 1:8)*

EARLY IN HIS FIRST LETTER TO TIMOTHY, the apostle Paul warns
the young evangelist of certain false teachers on the prowl in
Ephesus.

> As I urged you when I went into Macedonia—remain
> in Ephesus that you may charge some that they teach no
> other doctrine, nor give heed to fables and endless ge-
> nealogies, which cause disputes rather than godly edi-
> fication which is in faith. Now the purpose of the com-
> mandment is love from a pure heart, from a good
> conscience, and from sincere faith, from which some,
> having strayed, have turned aside to idle talk, desiring
> to be teachers of the law, understanding neither what
> they say nor the things which they affirm. (1 Tim. 1:3-7)

Immediately following this warning, verse 8 begins with the
affirmation, "But we know that the law is good if one uses it
lawfully," that is, not as the aforementioned false teachers have
used it. That affirmation sets forth the first theme of Paul's letter to this young preacher.

Erroneous and unlawful teaching of the law is still with us.

157

I am convinced that the present widespread contempt for civil laws is the inevitable outgrowth of disregard and disrespect for divine laws. Adding to this is the appalling ignorance in the church on this subject—the fruit of silence in the pulpit, or worse yet, false teaching.

At Stake—the Meaning of the Cross

False teaching on the law in the form of antinomianism robs the cross of its very foundation. The base of the cross is eternal justice, demonstrated in Christ's satisfying the just demands of God's holy law. The first message of the cross is not "God loves you," but "God's law has been broken." Viewing the cross without the law is like trying to assemble a jigsaw puzzle in thin air. With no base on which to connect the pieces, a clear picture of God's grace never takes shape. Yes, the spirit of the cross is eternal love, but the base of the cross is eternal justice. Preaching and teaching the law will save the gospel and Christianity from sentimentalism, emotionalism, and a superstitious perversion of the cross.

We must view the cross not only from the human side but also from the divine side. From the human side, we learn that God loved and demonstrated that love by giving His Son to die for sinners. From the divine side, we see God the Father thrusting the sword of divine justice into the heart of His Son.

The cross did not catch God by surprise. It was not an accident; it was part of the divine plan. "Him, being delivered by the determined counsel and foreknowledge of God, you have taken by lawless hands, have crucified, and put to death" (Acts 2:23). The apostles Peter and John reflected this truth in their prayer, "For truly against Your holy Servant Jesus, whom You anointed, both Herod and Pontius Pilate, with the Gentiles and the people of Israel, were gathered together to do whatever *Your* hand and *Your* purpose determined before to be done" (Acts 4:27-28).

Among the purposes of the cross was God's plan to "magnify the law and make it honorable" (Isa. 42:21). The cross does not make sense apart from the law.

An unbalanced emphasis on grace has led many people to neglect certain vital functions of the law. In its accusing and convicting function, the law is a schoolmaster to lead men to Christ. The absence of this dimension in preaching today has resulted in a truncated gospel, rushed "conversions," and shallow religious experience. The law prepares the way for the gospel. It is the sharp needle of the law that makes way for the scarlet thread of the gospel. Ignorance of the nature, design, and functions of the law is at the bottom of a great deal of religious error today (cf. 1 Tim. 1:7).

Throughout this book we have been trying to answer the following questions concerning the relationship of the law to the gospel.

1. Should someone who is under grace have regard for the law of God?
2. Is the person who is led by the Spirit obligated to keep the commandments?
3. To what kind of moral conduct does the Spirit lead a Christian?
4. Does the gospel nullify the law?
5. What function does God's law have in bringing lost sinners to Christ?
6. What function does God's law have in the Christian life?

In this chapter we shall give special attention to the proper function of God's law (5 and 6), along with some common misuses of the law.

1 Timothy 1:1–11

What does it mean to use the law "lawfully" (1 Tim. 1:8)? A brief commentary on verses 1–11 will help us answer that question.

The whole epistle to the young evangelist Timothy could be called Paul's Directory for the Church of God. In verses 3 and 4 the apostle gives his reason for writing. He tells Timothy to charge certain men not to teach different doctrine. Paul does not name names in verse 3, but later, in verse 20, he identifies Hymenaeus and Alexander.

The false teachers were propagating something new— a different doctrine. They had what has been called an "Athenian spirit." What is an Athenian spirit? It is described in Acts 17:21: "All the Athenians and the foreigners who were there spent their time in nothing else but either to tell or to hear some new thing." They were "novelty teachers." As I've mentioned before, a good rule of thumb is to beware of anyone who teaches what is contrary to the Ten Commandments, the Lord's Prayer, the Apostles' Creed. And so Paul warned Timothy of those who "give heed to fables and endless genealogies" (1 Tim. 1:4).

In verse 5 Paul gives the purpose of that commandment to oppose false teachers. The purpose is love, which can only come from a real experience of the grace of God. Paul gives a three-fold description of its source: It springs (1) from a pure heart, (2) from a good conscience, and (3) from sincere, unfeigned faith. Having strayed from these three evidences of grace, the false teachers have drawn others into profitless speculation and vain talk (v. 6).

In verse 7 we see that those who were in error wanted to be teachers of the law but had no insight into its meaning. Their teaching was born of stubborn ignorance.

It is in this context of Paul's opposition to false teaching concerning the law that we come upon verse 8: "But we know that the law is good if one uses it lawfully." Two observations that should strike us: (1) The law is good if a person uses it lawfully. (2) The law of God may be used unlawfully. And so, we need to focus on what those lawful and unlawful uses are.

Verse 8 begins with the strong affirmation, "We know . . ." One of my past mentors used to say:

- If a man does not know and thinks that he knows, he is a fool. Stay away from him.
- If a man does not know, and knows that he does not know, he is ignorant. Teach him.

• But when you find a man who knows, and knows that he knows, he is wise. Follow him.

Paul is that man. He says with full confidence, "We know that the law is good." What follows is not a comprehensive exposition of the law but, rather, a corrective statement concerning particular abuses of it by false teachers. Paul, of course, has much more to say about the law than he says here.

In this passage he says that "the law is not made for a righteous person" (v. 9). Before explaining what he means, let me state emphatically what verse 9 does not mean. It does not mean that the Christian has nothing to do with the law, or that the law has nothing to do with the Christian.

Paul begins verse 8 by contrasting what "we know" with what the false teachers do not understand (vv. 6-7). "We know that the law is good." He goes on to indicate that the law must be handled lawfully (not mishandled or abrogated). What law is Paul talking about in 1 Timothy 1:1–11? He obviously has in mind the moral law. Space does not allow us to demonstrate all the evidence that the moral law is intended. The list of sins in verses 9–10 should be enough to establish that. Those sins follow the same order as the second table of the Ten Commandments (cf. Ex. 20:12–16). It would be natural for Paul, with his training in the law, to follow that order. (Compare this list with his lists in Rom. 13:8–10 and 1 Cor. 6:9–10. They also follow the order of the Ten Commandments.)

In order for the law to accomplish its proper intent, it must be used lawfully, the way our Creator intended it to be used. But 1 Timothy 1:9 mentions that the law is not made for the righteous. Who are the righteous in the world? They are Christians in the process of being conformed to the moral requirements of their Creator, objectively set out in the Ten Commandments. This is being accomplished by the work of Christ wrought in them by the Holy Spirit: ". . . that the righteous requirements of the law might be fulfilled in us who do not walk according to the flesh but according to the Spirit" (Rom. 8:4).

We must always remember that the law was written on

Adam's heart when he was righteous and innocent. It did not curse or condemn before Adam sinned. We must also remember that the angels were under law, otherwise they could not have sinned. "Where there is no law there is no transgression" (Rom. 4:15). ". . . God did not spare the angels who sinned, but cast them down to hell and delivered them into chains of darkness, to be reserved for judgment . . ." (2 Peter 2:4).

The picture we get from 1 Timothy 1 is that the law is good, but difficult to teach and subject to misuse. Just as it is hard to teach free will without denying free grace, or to teach free grace without denying responsibility, likewise it is hard to give the law its due and not seem to prejudice the gospel, or to teach the gospel and not prejudice the law.

Unlawful Uses of the Law

When is the law used unlawfully?

1. It is an unlawful use when it is misinterpreted as it was by the scribes and Pharisees.
2. It is unlawfully used when it is set up as opposed to Christ, opposed to grace, or opposed to the gospel—one of the errors of the Jews.
3. The most dangerous and damning unlawful use is when men look to the law for justification—seeking acceptance before God by law keeping. This overthrows the very nature of grace, opposes Christ in His fullness, and overthrows justification by faith alone.
4. It is an unlawful use of the law to use it to discourage the brokenhearted sinners. This is why the law and the gospel must be preached together.
5. It is an unlawful use of the law to overthrow the grace of hope (cf. Rom. 5.)
6. It is an unlawful use of the law to take away the glory due to God in the great and marvelous work of justification.
7. It is an unlawful use of the law to overthrow the doctrine of sanctification. There is no power in the law to

justify or sanctify. The power must come from the Spirit. That is why we must never separate the Spirit from the law or gospel. Each will be powerless without the Spirit.

8. It is an unlawful use of the law to use it merely as ammunition in unfruitful and unprofitable disputes. If preachers and teachers do not teach Christ by the law, it is an unlawful use of the law.

How the Law Is Good

Our text says the law is good if it is used lawfully. The law is good in respect to the *matter* or *content* found in the Ten Commandments. All Christian duty can be traced to the Ten Commandments, as can all sin.

The commandments are good concerning the *authority* stamped upon them by God, whereby they have become a rule of life for us. We see in Matthew 5 that our Savior does not abrogate the law but shows the comprehensive authority of the law over spiritual issues far beyond the Pharisees' expectation.

The law is good because it is the *instrument* that the Spirit of God uses to convict of sin and to quicken believers to duty. "You have quickened me by Your precepts" (Ps. 119:50). It is unreasonable to separate the law of God from the Spirit of God. Paul said in Romans 7:14 that "the law is spiritual."

The law is good in respect to its *acts*.

- It acts to declare the will of God for moral conduct.
- It acts to command obedience to the will of God.
- It acts to invite by promise—or to compel by threats.
- It acts to condemn transgressors.

The law is good in respect to its *end* or *purpose*, which is Christ. We have a noble calling, proving that the law in all its parts aims to bring us into conformity to Christ. It has the righteousness of Christ as its scope.

Some Lawful Uses of the Law

When is the law used lawfully?

1. The law is used lawfully when it is used to inform all creatures—Christian and non-Christian—of the nature and will of God. The law stems from His nature, reflecting in its perfection the perfection of God. "The law of the LORD is perfect, converting the soul" (Ps. 19:7).
2. The law is used lawfully when it informs all creatures of their duty to God and man.
3. The law is used lawfully when it binds all creatures to walk according to the Creator's revealed will.
4. The law is used lawfully when it is used to convince believers and unbelievers of their inability to keep it apart from the Spirit.
5. The law is used lawfully when it is used to convince men, women, and children of the sinful pollution of their natures, hearts, and lives, thus driving them to Christ for forgiveness.
6. The law is used lawfully when it is used to humble men and women in the sense of their sins and misery.
7. The law is used lawfully when it is used to help men and women to a clearer sight of their need of Christ and the perfection of His obedience.
8. The law is used lawfully when it helps men and women to have proper esteem for the matchless character of Christ.

The Use of the Law Peculiar to Christians
A special use of the law among Christians is that it makes Christ more precious to us. He perfectly obeyed all of its precepts for us. This shows us how much we are bound to Him for doing what we could not do, both in His life and in His death. "For He made Him who knew no sin to be sin for us, that we might become the righteousness of God in Him" (2 Cor. 5:21). Knowing this produces love and thankfulness.

The Use of the Law for Non-Christians

1. It is a lawful use of the law when it is used to restrain the spirits of wicked men. A great old Puritan Samuel Bolton said,

Blessed be God that there is this fear upon the spirits of wicked men; otherwise we could not well live in the world. One man would be a devil to another. Every man would be a Cain to his brother, an Ammon to his sister, an Absolom to his father, a Saul to himself, a Judas to his master; for what one man does, all men would do, were it not for a restraint upon their spirits. (*True Bounds of Christian Freedom* [London: Banner of Truth, 1964], 79)

The Ten Commandments curb evil in the world.

2. It is a lawful use of the law when it is used to inform sinners of their duty to God and man. The law condemns and convinces the unconverted of their sin and misery.
3. It is a lawful use of the law when it is used to render sinners inexcusable if they reject God's promise and remedy in Christ. "For since the creation of the world His invisible attributes are clearly seen, being understood by the things that are made, even His eternal power and Godhead, so that they are without excuse" (Rom. 1:20).

The commandments were originally written perfectly on Adam's heart, and he had perfect, sufficient knowledge of the Creator's will, as well as the power to obey. Although this clear view of the law was defaced by the Fall, it was not totally obliterated. Romans 2:14–15 teach us that some faint impressions of the law still remain on the hearts of reasonable men. On Mount Sinai, God was graciously pleased to give a new, written copy of the moral law, summed up in the Ten Commandments.

WE HAVE SEEN that when one becomes a Christian, a new creation, God writes that same perfect law on the heart. The one who makes good and lawful use of the law is the person who has Christ and grace in his heart as well. It is he who can sing with the psalmist, "Oh, how I love Your law!" (Ps. 119:97).

CHAPTER SIXTEEN

The Gospel, Our Trust

*"We have been approved by God to be entrusted
with the gospel. . . ." (1 Thess. 2:4)*

*"According to the glorious gospel of the blessed God which
was committed to my trust." (1 Tim. 1:11)*

THE TWO VERSES QUOTED ABOVE teach us that we are trustees of
the glorious gospel of God. It is an awesome responsibility to
be a trustee, a steward of that divinely inspired message, which
has to do with life and death, yes, heaven and hell. As long as
there is sin in the world, as long as men die, the divinely inspired message will be very relevant.

No one in this world needs help as much as those who lack
the gospel. They lack everything that would do them good. A
throne without the gospel is a devil's dungeon. Wealth without the gospel is fuel for hell. All building without the gospel
is building on sand.

Every true minister and every true Christian longs to see a revival of true religion that will affect personal conduct, piety in
the home, and the social and moral standards in the community.
It is my deep conviction that such a revival will not be seen unless there is a recovery of the gospel of the grace of God. True
revival will not come by some new methods of church growth
or more religious machinery or more conventions or more sym-
posiums or conferences. It will only come by the powerful
preaching of the divinely inspired message we call the gospel,
that gospel which no human mind could conceive or invent.

In 1 Thessalonians 2:1–12, that gospel, designated as our trust, is twice called the gospel of God. It is the message that saves souls and builds New Testament churches. It is what the great apostle preached: "I declare to you the gospel which I preached to you, which also you received and in which you stand, by which also you are saved, if you hold fast that word which I preached to you—unless you believed in vain" (1 Cor. 15:1–2).

What Is the Gospel?

John Brown offers the best definition of the gospel that I have found.

> The Saxon word Gospel, like the Greek word of which it is a literal translation, signifies agreeable intelligence, a joyful announcement, good news, glad tidings; and is, in the New Testament, ordinarily employed as a descriptive designation of the revelation of Divine mercy to our lost world,—the divinely inspired account of the only way in which guilty, depraved, and miserable men may be delivered from sin and its consequences, obtain the Divine approbation and favor, be raised to the true dignity and excellence of their intellectual and moral nature in the knowledge of God and conformity to His mind and will, and be made happy in all the variety, and to the full extent, of their capacities of enjoyment, and during the whole eternity of their being, by the free grace of God, and "through the redemption that is in Christ Jesus." (John Brown, *The Resurrection of Life: An Exposition of 1 Cor. XV* [Edinburgh: William Oliphant and Sons, 1851])

There is power in this gospel, "the power of God to salvation" (Rom. 1:16) to make "everyone who believes" be what he or she is meant to be. No tidings were ever so joyful as those announced in the gospel, and no benefits were so good as those exhibited in it.

There is an appalling ignorance in the world as to just what the gospel is and what it does when it is savingly received. This ignorance also exists among church people. Let me illustrate from a personal experience.

Years ago when I was president of a small construction company, I had three women call on me one Monday morning. The receptionist tried to direct them to someone else in the office; however, they insisted on seeing me. My secretary prevailed upon me to see them. When I reached the front office, sure enough, there were three nice ladies. They said they were from a local church. They wanted to sell me a cookbook (not very useful in the construction business). They had heard I was religious and was a sure touch for a contribution. I soon learned that I was about to buy a cookbook and I thought I might at least inquire what the church was going to do with the proceeds. They were not quite sure what the money was going to be used for, so I thought I would help them with an answer. "It would be a good idea to use the money to spread the gospel." My suggestion was met with perfect unanimity—they all thought it was a good idea to use the money to spread the gospel. Then, to be sure, I asked them, "What is the gospel?" Their answers underscore the prevailing ignorance in the church. The first woman said, "The gospel is the Ten Commandments"; the second one said, "It is a symbol of Christ"; the third said, "It is the golden rule"—to which responses I was prompted to asked if they were all members of the same church!

The word *gospel* is used at least ninety times in the New Testament. Mark calls it "the gospel of Jesus Christ" (Mark 1:1) and "the gospel of the kingdom of God" (Mark 1:14). This gospel must first be preached to all nations before the end (Mark 13:10). It is also called "the gospel of peace" (Eph. 6:15), "the gospel of the grace of God" (Acts 20:24), "the gospel of your salvation" (Eph. 1:13), and "the everlasting gospel" (Rev. 14:6).

Generally the phrase "the gospel" is used variously to mean:

- the teachings of Christ and His apostles.
- the history of Christ's birth, death, resurrection, and ascension.
- the preaching of the Word of Christ, particularly, the doctrines and offers of salvation through Him.

But the gospel, in its strict and proper meaning, signifies good news, glad tidings, joyful announcement in the form of a divinely inspired message. That message contains information needing explanation and application, and it includes invitation.

The gospel is a message communicated in words, but not in words only. "For our gospel did not come to you in word only, but also in power, in the Holy Spirit and in much assurance, as you know what kind of men we were among you for your sake" (1 Thess. 1:5).

For my purposes in this chapter, I will confine my thoughts to the gospel message in its strict and proper meaning. This message has four ingredients, all of which must be present in order to have the biblical gospel. (The substance for these four ingredients is taken from J. I. Packer, *Evangelism and the Sovereignty of God* [Downers Grove, Ill.: InterVarsity, 1961].)

Four Essential Ingredients

The First Ingredient: God

The gospel is a divinely inspired message about God. This ingredient is often overlooked or partly omitted. It is about God the Creator and Judge of all the earth and our relationship to Him, that is, the Creator-creature relationship. As Creator He has absolute claim on us creatures. We must know what He requires of His creatures. The Creator-creature relationship must be established before the Redeemer-redeemed relationship will make sense.

Jesus came to reconcile us to God. The gospel is a message about *God*. It tells us who He is, what His character is, what His standards are, and what He requires of us, His creatures. It tells us that we owe our very existence to Him, that for good or ill we are always in His hands and under His eye, and that He made us to worship and serve Him, to show forth His praise and to live for His glory. These truths are the foundation of theistic religion. Until they are grasped the rest of the gospel message will seem neither cogent nor relevant. It is here, with the assertion of man's complete and constant dependence on his Creator, that the Christian story begins.

We can learn again from Paul at this point. When preaching to Jews, as at Pisidian Antioch, he did not need to mention the fact that men were God's creatures; he could take this knowledge for granted, for his hearers had the Old Testament faith behind them. He could begin at once to declare Christ to them, as the fulfillment of Old Testament hopes. But when preaching to Gentiles, who knew nothing of the Old Testament, Paul had to go further back, and start from the beginning. And the beginning from which Paul started in such cases was the doctrine of God's creatorship and man's creaturehood. So, when the Athenians asked him to explain what his talk of Jesus and the resurrection was all about, he spoke to them first of God the Creator, and why He made man: "God . . . made the world. . . . He gives to all life, breath, and all things. And has made . . . every nation . . . that they should seek the Lord" (Acts 17:24-27). This was not, as some have supposed, a piece of philosophical apologetic of a kind that Paul afterwards renounced, but the first and basic lesson in theistic faith.

The gospel starts by teaching us that we, as creatures, are absolutely dependent on God, and that He, as Creator, has an absolute claim on us. Only when we have learned this can we see what sin is, and only when we see what sin is can we understand the good news of salvation from sin. We must know what it means to call God Creator before we can grasp what it means to speak of Him as Redeemer. Nothing can be achieved by talking about sin and salvation where this preliminary lesson has not in some measure been learned.

The Second Ingredient: Sin

The gospel is a divinely inspired message about sin. When we ask, What is sin? immediately we are faced with the law—the Ten Commandments. "Whoever commits sin also commits lawlessness, and sin is lawlessness" (1 John 3:4). By the law is the knowledge of sin. The first message of the cross is Christ's satisfying divine justice; the very base of the cross has to do with eternal justice.

This is why in days gone by parents taught their children the Ten Commandments. In the catechism the children learned the Ten Commandments, not because they thought they would be saved by keeping the commandments, but because the commandments would show them their need to be saved by the matchless grace of Christ.

It is interesting to note in reading the life of John Paton, the great Presbyterian missionary to the New Hebrides, that the first thing he taught the pagans was not John 3:16, but rather the Ten Commandments. The same thing was true of John Elliot, the first missionary to the American Indians. His first sermon to the Indians was the Ten Commandments. We might ask Why? The answer is very clear: that they would be made conscious of their sin against their Creator and see their need of a Savior. Sin is the transgression of the law. Jesus is a Savior from sin, not just from the consequences of sin. We learn this from the very first chapter in the New Testament: "She will bring forth a Son, and you shall call His name JESUS, for He will save His people from their sins" (Matt. 1:21). Notice, it does not say save His people *in* their sins, but *from* their sins. This divinely inspired message is about sin—not just life's casualties.

In the Bible the very idea of sin is that it is an offense against God, which disrupts a man's relationship with God. Unless we see our shortcomings in the light of the law and the holiness of God, we do not see them as *sin* at all. For sin is not a social concept; it is a theological concept. Though sin is committed by man, and many sins are against society, sin cannot be defined in terms of either man or society. We never know what sin really is until we have learned to think of it in terms of God, and to measure it not by human standards but by the yardstick of His total demand on our lives.

What we have to grasp, then, is that the bad conscience of the natural man is not at all the same thing as conviction of sin. It does not, therefore, follow that a man is convicted of sin when he is distressed about his weaknesses and the wrong things he has done. It is not conviction of sin just to feel miserable about yourself and your failures and your inadequacy to meet life's demands. Nor would it be saving faith if a man in that condition called on the Lord Jesus Christ just to soothe him and cheer him up and make him feel confident again. Nor would we be preaching the gospel (though we might imagine we were) if all we did was to present Christ in terms of a man's felt wants. ("Are you happy? Are you satisfied? Do you want peace of mind? Do you feel that you have failed? Are you fed up with yourself? Do you want a friend? Then come to Christ; He will meet your every need . . ."—as if the Lord Jesus Christ were a fairy godmother or a super-psychiatrist.) No, we have to go deeper than that. To preach sin means not to make capital out of people's felt frailties (the brainwasher's trick) but to measure their lives by the holy law of God. To be convicted of sin means not just to feel that one is an all-round flop but to realize that one has offended God, and flouted His authority, and defiled Him, and gone against Him, and put oneself in the wrong with Him. To preach Christ means to set Him forth as the One who through His cross sets men right with God again. To put faith in Christ means relying on Him, and Him alone, to restore us to God's fellowship and favor.

It is indeed true that the real Christ, the Christ of the Bible, who offers Himself to us as a Savior from sin and an Advocate with God, does in fact give peace, and joy, and moral strength, and the privilege of His own friendship to those who trust Him. But the Christ who is depicted and desired merely to ease life's casualties and make us more comfortable is not the real Christ. He is a misrepresented and misconceived Christ—in effect, an imaginary Christ. And if we teach people to look to an imaginary Christ, we have no grounds for expecting that they will find real salvation. We must be on our guard, therefore, against equating a natural bad conscience and sense of wretchedness with spiritual conviction of sin, and so failing to impress upon sinners the basic truth about their condition— namely, that their sin has alienated them from God and exposed them to His condemnation, hostility, and wrath, so that their first need is for a restored relationship with Him.

It may be asked, What are the signs of true conviction of sin, as distinct from the mere smart of a bad conscience, or the mere disgust at life that any disillusioned person may feel? There seem to be three signs.

1. Conviction of sin is essentially *an awareness of a wrong relationship with God:* not just with one's neighbor or one's own conscience and ideals for oneself, but with one's Maker, the God in whose hand one's breath is and on whom one depends for existence every moment. To define conviction of sin as a sense of need, without qualification, would not be enough; it is not just any sense of need, but a sense of a particular need—a need for restoration of fellowship with God. It is the realization that, as one stands at present, one is in a relationship with God that spells only rejection, retribution, wrath, and pain, for the present and the future; and a realization that this is an intolerable relationship to remain in, and therefore a desire that, at whatever cost and on whatever terms, it might be changed. Conviction of sin may center upon the sense of one's guilt before God, or one's uncleanness in His sight, or one's rebellion against Him, or one's alienation and estrangement from Him. But always it is a sense of the need to get right, not simply with oneself or other people, but with God.

2. Conviction of sin always includes *conviction of sins:* a sense of guilt for particular wrongs done in the sight of God, from which one needs to turn and be rid of them, if he or she is ever to be right with God. Thus Isaiah was convicted specifically of sins of speech (Isa. 6:5), and Zacchaeus of sins of extortion (Luke 19:8).

3. Conviction of sin always includes *conviction of sinfulness:* a sense of one's complete corruption and perversity in God's

sight, and one's consequent need of what Ezekiel called a "new heart" (Ezek. 36:26) and our Lord called "a new birth," that is, a moral recreation. Thus, the author of Psalm 51—traditionally identified with David, under conviction of his sin with Bathsheba—confesses not only particular transgressions (vv. 1-4) but also the depravity of his nature (vv. 5-6), and seeks cleansing from the guilt and defilement of both (vv. 7-10). Indeed, perhaps the shortest way to tell whether a person is convicted of sin is to take him through Psalm 51 and see whether his heart resonates to the language of the psalmist.

The Third Ingredient: Christ

The gospel is a divinely inspired message about Christ, not any Christ, or one conceived by imagination or contrived by your own mind. There are many, many Christs on the religious market, but there is only one true biblical Christ. He is the one who came by a virgin's womb, suffered and died vicariously on a Roman cross, rose victoriously from a borrowed grave—and now has been exalted to a throne and wears the victor's crown. He is the Almighty's authorized Prophet, Priest, and King of His church. We must ask: Who is He? What did He do? Why did He do it? And where is He now?

Two points need to be made about how we declare this part of the message.

1. *We must not present the person of Christ apart from His saving work.* It is sometimes said that it is the presentation of Christ's person, rather than of doctrines about Him, that draws sinners to His feet. It is true that it is the living Christ who saves, and that a theory of the atonement, however orthodox, is no substitute. This remark usually implies, however, that doctrinal instruction is dispensable in evangelistic preaching, and that all the evangelist need do is paint a vivid word-picture of the Man of Galilee who went about doing good, and then assure his hearers that this Jesus is still alive to help them in their troubles. But such a message could hardly be called the gospel. It would, in reality, be a mere conundrum, serving only to mystify. Who was this Jesus? we should ask, and What is His posi-

tion now? Such preaching would raise these questions while concealing the answers, and thus it would completely baffle the thoughtful listener.

The truth is that you cannot make sense of the historic figure of Jesus until you know about the *incarnation*—that this Jesus was in fact God the Son made man to save sinners according to His Father's eternal purpose. Nor can you make sense of His life until you know about the *atonement*—that He lived as man so that He might die as man for men, and that His passion, His judicial murder, was really His saving act of bearing away the sins of the world. Nor can you tell on what terms to approach Him now until you know about His *resurrection, ascension,* and *heavenly session*—that Jesus has been raised, enthroned, and made King, and now lives to save to the uttermost all who acknowledge His lordship.

These doctrines, to mention no others, are essential to the gospel. Without them, there is no gospel, only a puzzle story about a man named Jesus. To regard the teaching of doctrines about Christ as opposed to the presenting of His person is, therefore, to put asunder two things that God has joined. It is really very perverse. Indeed, for the whole purpose of teaching these doctrines is to throw light on the person of the Lord Jesus Christ and to make clear to our hearers just who it is that we want them to meet. In ordinary social life, when we want people to know whom we are introducing, we tell them something about him and what he has done. And so it is here. The apostles themselves preached these doctrines in order to preach Christ, as the New Testament shows. In fact, without these doctrines, you have no gospel to preach at all.

2. *Likewise, we must not present the saving work of Christ apart from His person.* Preachers and personal workers have sometimes been known to make this mistake. In their concern to focus attention on the atoning death of Christ as the sole sufficient ground on which sinners may be accepted with God, they have expounded the summons to saving faith in these terms: "Believe that Christ died for your sins." The effect of this exposition is to represent the saving work of Christ in the past—

dissociated from His person in the present—as the whole object of our trust. But it is not biblical to isolate the work from the Worker. Nowhere in the New Testament is the call to believe expressed in such terms.

What the New Testament calls for is faith in Christ Himself, trust in the living Savior, who died for our sins. Thus, strictly speaking, the object of saving faith is not the atonement but the Lord Jesus Christ who made atonement. We must not, in presenting the gospel, isolate the cross and its benefits from the Christ whose cross it was. For the persons to whom the benefits of Christ's death belong are just those who trust His person and believe not simply on His saving death but on *Him*, the loving Savior. Paul said, "Believe on the *Lord Jesus Christ*, and you will be saved, you and your household" (Acts 16:31). Our Lord said, "Come to Me . . . and I will give you rest" (Matt. 11:28).

This being so, one thing becomes immediately clear. The question about the extent of the atonement, much agitated in some quarters, has no bearing on the content of the evangelistic message at this particular point. I am not asking here whether Christ died in order to save every single human being, past, present, and future. Nor am I inviting you now to make up your mind on this question if you have not done so already.

Obviously, if a preacher did not believe that Christ died for everyone, his gospel preaching would not say that Christ did. You do not find such a statement in the sermons of George Whitefield or Charles Spurgeon, for instance.

But even if an evangelist believes that Jesus died for all people, he need never say so when preaching the gospel. For preaching the gospel, as we have just seen, means inviting every sinner to come to Jesus Christ, the living Savior, not describing the extent of the atonement. The truth is that Christ, by virtue of His atoning death, is able to forgive and save all those who put their trust in Him. What has to be said about the cross when preaching the gospel is simply that Christ's death is the ground on which Christ's forgiveness is given. And this is all that has to be said. The question of the designed extent of the atonement does not come into the story at this point.

The New Testament never calls on any man to repent on the ground that Christ died specifically and particularly for him. The basis on which the New Testament invites sinners to put faith in Christ is simply that *they need Him,* and that *He offers Himself to them,* and that *those who receive Him are promised all the benefits that His death secured for His people.* What is universal and all-inclusive in the New Testament is the invitation to faith and the promise of salvation to all who believe.

Our task in carrying out our trust is to reproduce as faithfully as possible the New Testament emphasis. To go beyond the New Testament, or to destroy its viewpoint or shift its stress is always wrong. The New Testament knows only of a living Christ, and all apostolic preaching of the gospel holds up the living Christ to sinners. But the living Christ is Christ who died, and He is never preached apart from His death and its reconciling power. It is *the living Christ, by virtue of His reconciling death,* who is the burden of the apostolic message. The task of carrying out our trust is to preach *Christ . . . in His character as the Crucified.* The gospel is not, "believe that Christ died for everybody's sins, and therefore for yours," any more than it is "believe that Christ died only for certain people's sins, and so perhaps not for yours." The gospel is, "believe on the Lord Jesus Christ, who died for sins, and offers Himself to be your Savior." This is the message we are to take to the world. We have no business to ask them to put faith in any view of the extent of the atonement. Our job is to point them to the living Christ and summon them to trust in Him.

It was because they both grasped this that John Wesley and George Whitefield could regard each other as brothers in evangelism, though they differed on the extent of the atonement. Their views on this subject did not enter into their gospel preaching. Both were content to preach the gospel just as it stands in Scripture. They proclaimed the living Christ to sinners and invited the lost to come to Him, through whose death there is life.

The divinely inspired message must *always* contain His person and the doctrines about Him. We have all met those who are so doctrinally sound that they are sound asleep. They are as doctrinally straight as a gun barrel and just as empty. To avoid this, the divinely inspired message must be His person and His work.

The Fourth Ingredient: Faith and Repentance

The gospel is a divinely inspired summons to faith and repentance.

A summons is a call by authority to appear at a named place. It is a call to a duty. We summon an ambulance; we summon a fire truck; we summon the police. We do not call 911 and say, "Would you like to come to this terrible accident?" We do not call the fire department saying, "Would you please consider coming to this terrible fire?" No, when we call the police, firemen, or ambulance, it is an appeal to their duty, not an option.

In our civil law, a summons is a citation to appear in court. It is a written notification signed by the proper authority and served on the person to appear in court at a certain, specified place, day, and time.

Likewise, in the Scriptures a summons is not optional. The call to faith and repentance is a call to duty, a call issued with the voice of authority. It is given in the imperative mood.

When the people of Capernaum asked our Lord, "What shall we do, that we may work the works of God?" He answered, "This is the work of God, that you believe in Him whom He sent" (John 6:28-29). John put it like this: "And this is His *commandment:* that we should believe on the name of His Son Jesus Christ . . ." (1 John 3:23). In both of these passages we have a summons, a command to believe—a summons to faith.

The apostle Paul also issued a summons to the Athenians: "God . . . *commands* all men everywhere to repent" (Acts 17:30). Thus we see that the fourth ingredient of the gospel is a summons to faith and repentance.

Although repentance is missing from much evangelistic preaching today, Jesus unmistakably preached repentance: "Now after John was put in prison, Jesus came to Galilee, preaching the gospel of the kingdom of God, and saying, 'The time is fulfilled, and the kingdom of God is at hand. Repent, and believe in the gospel'" (Mark 1:14–15). The apostles also preached repentance: "So they went out and preached that people should repent" (Mark 6:12). Jesus taught His followers that remission of sins was inseparably linked to repentance: ". . . repentance and remission of sins should be preached in His name to all nations, beginning at Jerusalem" (Luke 24:47). Peter preached repentance: "Then Peter said to them, 'Repent, and let every one of you be baptized in the name of Jesus Christ for the remission of sins; and you shall receive the gift of the Holy Spirit'" (Acts 2:38); "Repent therefore and be converted" (Acts 3:19). Paul, reviewing a three-year ministry with the Ephesian elders, reminded them that repentance was an ingredient in the gospel he preached: "I kept back nothing that was helpful, but proclaimed it to you, and taught you publicly and from house to house, testifying to Jews, and also to Greeks, repentance toward God and faith toward our Lord Jesus Christ" (Acts 20:20-21).

Faith and Repentance Inseparable

In response to these and many other passages, the question is often raised, Why, when the Bible speaks of forgiveness of sin and eternal life, does it sometimes just say "believe," sometimes, "repent," and still other times, both?

The answer to this question is found in the definition of *repentance* found in the Westminster Shorter Catechism.

> Q. 87. *What is repentance unto life?*
> A. Repentance unto life is a saving grace, whereby a sinner, out of a true sense of his sin, and apprehension of the mercy of God in Christ, doth, with grief and hatred of his sin, turn from it unto God, with full purpose of, and endeavor after, new obedience.

Notice that repentance is not only turning from sin to Christ, but also the apprehension of the mercy of God in Christ—that is, faith. This teaches us that faith and repentance are Siamese twins—inseparably joined together in God's salvation. Where there is true faith, there will always be evangelical repentance; and where there is evangelical repentance, there will always be saving faith.

There is spurious faith and a legal repentance that do not apprehend the mercy of God in Christ. A clear example of this is found by comparing Peter and Judas. The Bible says Judas repented and then went out and hanged himself. Judas did not embrace the mercy of God in Christ. His kiss of betrayal was not a greater sin than Peter's curse of denial, but Peter did not hang himself. After his denial, Peter remembered the words of Jesus and wept bitterly. He clearly embraced the mercy of God in Christ.

The answer to our question Why does the Bible sometimes just say "believe," other times just "repent," and sometimes both? is that they are inseparably joined together in the application of God's salvation. Thus, in every case, the Bible is calling for the same response.

True repentance is always consistent with true faith. Spurious repentance dwells on the consequences of sin rather than on sin itself. I have known some sinners so disturbed with the fears of hell and thoughts of death and eternal judgment that, to use the words of one old preacher, "They have been shaking over the mouth of hell by their collar, and have almost felt the torments of the pit before they went there." Such fears may come with true repentance, but they are not the essential part of repentance. As John Bunyan in his *Holy War* has well said, "Diabolus often beats the great hell-drum in the ears of Mansoul, to prevent their hearing the trumpet of the gospel which proclaims mercy and pardon."

Any repentance that keeps a sinner from believing in Christ is a repentance that needs to be repented of. Any repentance that makes a sinner think Christ will not save him goes beyond the truth of the Bible. Yes, it goes *against* the truth. Any repentance that leads to despair and remorse but does not embrace mercy is a repentance of the Devil and not of God.

A person may feel he has done wrong but go on sinning all the same, feeling that there is no hope and that he may as well continue seeking the pleasures of sin since he cannot, so he thinks, have the pleasures of grace and forgiveness. That is spurious repentance. It is the fire of the Devil, which hardens the heart in sin, and not the Lord's fire of mercy, which melts the heart in repentance. In Peter's repentance, he wept bitterly, yet embraced the mercy of God in Christ. One old Puritan, on his sick bed, expressed it this way: "Lord, sink me low as hell in repentance; but lift me high as heaven in faith."

To put it yet another way, true repentance is to sorrow bitterly for sin you know should damn you, but to rejoice greatly in Christ as if the sin were nothing at all. Repentance strips a person of self-righteousness, and faith clothes him with Christ. Repentance purges the soul of dead works, and faith fills the soul with living works. Repentance pulls down, and faith builds up. Repentance orders a time to weep, and faith gives a time to dance. Together these two make up the work of grace within, whereby men's souls are saved.

The repentance we ought to preach is one connected with faith. Thus, we may preach repentance and faith together without any difficulty whatsoever. Like twins, they are born at the same time. To say which is first is beyond my knowledge. They come to the soul together, and we must preach them together.

Spurgeon said, "So then, dear friends, those people who have faith which allows them to think lightly of past sin, have the faith of devils and not the faith of God's elect."

Our need to repent and believe continues until our dying day. Rowland Hill, when he was near death, said he had one regret, and that was that a dear friend who lived with him for sixty years would have to leave him at the gate of heaven. "That dear friend," said he, "is repentance; repentance has been with me all my life, and I think I shall drop a tear as I go through the gates to think that I can repent no more."

First Thessalonians 1:9 sets forth three things that happen in every true conversion to some degree: "They [believers in Macedonia and Achaia] themselves declare concerning us what manner of entry we had to you, and how you turned to God from idols to serve the living and true God." Paul says that the Thessalonians (1) turned to God (faith) and (2) turned from idols (from sin—repentance) (3) to serve the living and true God (evidence of repentance).

At the center of these three responses, and inseparable from faith and good works, is repentance. Repentance and faith are sacred duties and twin graces wrought in our souls by the regenerating Spirit of God, whereby, being deeply convicted of our guilt, danger, helplessness, and of the way of salvation by Christ, we turn to God with unfeigned contrition, confession, and supplication for mercy; at the same time heartily receiving the Lord Jesus Christ as our Prophet, Priest, and King, and relying on Him alone as the only and all-sufficient Savior.

Law and Gospel Inseparable

We have seen that the gospel is a divinely inspired message about God, about sin, and about Christ, and a summons to faith and repentance.

If repentance and faith are inseparable, then the law and the gospel are likewise inseparable. What I mean is that anyone who is an enemy of the law is also an enemy of the gospel. And no one can be an enemy to the gospel without being, at the same time, an enemy to the law. Every enemy to the gospel is, in the same degree, an enemy to the perfection, spirituality, and honor of the law.

The law and the gospel are in such harmony with each other as to have no divided interests. Therefore, someone who is destitute of unfeigned love for the doctrines and promises of the gospel, however strict his profession of religion may be, is really an *antinomian*, an enemy to the honor of the holy law. He is also an adversary to the honor of the law if by rejecting the spotless righteousness of Jesus Christ tendered to him in the gospel, he refuses to present the *only* righteousness, by which the law can be magnified and made honorable. He is an enemy, likewise, to the authority and honor of the law as a *rule of duty*. For by his disbelief of the promises of the blessed gospel, he refuses to receive that grace from the fullness of Christ, without which he cannot honor the law by so much as a single act of acceptable obedience.

If a person has experienced a saving knowledge of the gospel, he or she will undoubtedly *evidence it* by obedience of heart and life to the law in the hand of Christ as a rule of duty. People can never perform holy obedience to the law so long as they remain ignorant of the gospel. But when they begin spiritually to discern the truth, suitableness, and glory of the doctrine of redeeming grace, they will then begin to perform spiritual and sincere obedience to the law of Christ as a rule. "He died for all [who were given Him by the Father] that those who live should live no longer for themselves, but for Him who died for them and rose again" (2 Cor. 5:15). When someone spiritually discerns and sincerely loves the grace of the gospel, he at the same time sees and loves the holiness of the law. The consequence will be that he will sincerely and cheerfully desire to obey the law. He will yield this obedience not only because the authority of God obliges him and the love of Christ constrains him, but also because he discerns the beauty of the holiness of the law itself and loves it.

A true believer is, in proportion as he is sanctified, rich in faith and in good works. Although the exercise of graces and the performance of duties gain nothing for the believer at the hand of God, yet they themselves are unspeakably great gain to him. He counts it a privilege and a pleasure to have duties to perform, and to have a disposition given him to perform them to the glory of his God and Savior. For, as there can be no happiness without holiness, so too the believer is comfortable and happy in proportion as he is holy. The more he believes and applies the gospel, trusting cordially in the Lord Jesus for his salvation, and the more his faith works by love, so much the more communion with Christ and enjoyment of God are his infinite portion. The legalist expects happiness *for* his duties, but the true believer enjoys happiness *in* them.

What Always Accompanies Saving Faith?

The answer to that question is found in the most succinct definition of a Christian in all the Bible: "Therefore, if anyone is in

Christ he is a new creation; old things have passed away; behold, all things have become new" (2 Cor. 5:17). This little verse speaks of three characteristics of the person who has saving faith.

In Christ: The Essence of True Religion
The expression "in Christ" is used 240 times in the New Testament. Indeed, it is the essence of true religion. If I could ask only one question to help a person determine his relationship to his Maker, it would be this: *Are you in Christ?* Everything God has for you is *in Christ!* "Of Him you are in Christ Jesus, who became for us wisdom from God—and righteousness and sanctification and redemption" (1 Cor. 1:30).

- In Christ is our justification.
- In Christ is our sanctification.
- In Christ is our adoption.
- In Christ is our wisdom.
- In Christ is our righteousness.

"In Christ" signifies a personal relationship. It expresses the most exalted relationship that can exist—an inseparable relationship, an indestructible relationship, an unspeakable relationship that cannot be defined in word only.

New Creation: The Effects of True Religion
The second important truth found in 2 Corinthians 5:17 concerns the effects of regeneration: "new creation." Regeneration is the powerful, supernatural work of the triune God. God the Father planned our redemption; God the Son prayed for it (John 17) and purchased it; God the Spirit effectually applies it in regeneration.

We can explain *what* the Spirit does, but *how* He does it let no man pretend to know. "The wind blows where it wishes, and you hear the sound of it, but cannot tell where it comes from and where it goes. So is everyone who is born of the Spirit" (John 3:8). So it is with regeneration.

All Things New: The Evidence of True Religion

The third important truth found in 2 Corinthians 5:17 is the evidence of regeneration: "Old things have passed away; behold, all things have become new."

How does one know if he or she is regenerate? Regeneration is known by its effects. Regeneration always includes (1) the enlightening of the mind, (2) the convicting of the conscience, and (3) the renewing of the will. It is by the work of the Spirit that (1) the natural blindness is removed, (2) the natural enmity is subdued, and (3) the natural man becomes a new creature in all his views, feelings, desires, affections, aims, habits, and hopes.

This new creature enters into a new conflict in his soul. It is the conflict that Paul refers to in Romans 7, between the law in his members and the law of his mind. An unconverted person may be conscious of a conflict between sin and the conscience. But the new creature in Christ has a different conflict, that is, a conflict between sin and the will. The difference between the two (sin and conscience versus sin and the will) consists entirely in the position of the will. In the unconverted, the will is on the side of sin, and both are opposed to conscience. In the new creature, the will is on the side of conscience, and both are opposed to sin.

Finally, do the law and the gospel agree with and subserve the honor of each other? Most certainly. Then, let believers always take heed that they do not set them in opposition to one another. Beware, O believer, of ever setting the law in hostile opposition to the gospel, or the gospel in opposition to the law.

John Newton summarized it very well.

> Clearly to understand the distinction, connection, and harmony between the Law and the Gospel, and their mutual subserviency to illustrate and establish each

other, is a singular privilege, and a happy means of preserving the soul from being entangled by errors on the
right hand or on the left. (John Newton, *Works* [London:
Banner of Truth], 1:350)

Examination and Invitation

Do you desire to know whether you are "experimentally" (experientially) acquainted with the grace of the gospel? Pray that
the Lord may examine and test you, and then ask yourself some
questions: Do I know spiritually, and believe fervently, the doctrines of this glorious gospel? Do I spiritually discern the ex-
cellence and suitableness of the plan of redemption exhibited
in the gospel; and do I heartily approve, so far as I know them,
all the parts of that wonderful scheme? Do I eagerly comply
with the invitations and accept the offers of the gospel? Do I frequently endeavor to embrace and trust the promises of it, and
do I place the confidence of my heart in the Lord Jesus for *all*
the salvation promised in the gospel?

Do I love the gospel, so as to delight in reading and hearing
and meditating on it? Do I love and admire the gospel because
it is the doctrine, the only doctrine, that is "according to godliness," or because it is the only mirror in which believers so contemplate the glory of God in the face of Jesus Christ as to be
"changed into the same image from glory to glory, by the Spirit
of the Lord"? And do I find that, under the transforming and
consoling influence of the gospel, I in some measure delight in
the law of God according to the inward man, and run in the way
of *all* His commandments?

If you can answer these questions in the affirmative, you may
confidently conclude that you have attained, in some happy
measure, that supernatural and first-hand knowledge of the glorious gospel which is the beginning of eternal life in the soul, and
is inseparably connected with evangelical holiness in all manner
of your conduct. You accept your duty, in the faith of the promise,
to grow daily in grace and in the knowledge of our Lord and Savior Jesus Christ and never be moved away from the hope of the

gospel. But, if you cannot answer in the affirmative so much as one of these questions, you ought to conclude that you are yet a stranger to the grace of the gospel. And, instead of yielding to despair, you should, without delay, come as a sinner to the Lord Jesus, who is given for a light to the Gentiles.

Epilogue

Little needs to be said in conclusion, except to stress the obvious and sacred importance that God, in the Scripture, attaches to His holy law. This must be taken to heart by the believer and the preacher alike. The believer must increasingly delight in it "according to the inward man" (Rom. 7:22), demonstrating the truth of the Lord's saying, "If anyone loves Me, he will keep My word" (John 14:23). The preacher, likewise, must seek the help of the Holy Spirit so that in his preaching, he honors the law, and as he expounds the law, he sends men to the gospel. It brings no praise to God when either of these glorious manifestations of His ways is neglected.

As a memory aid to their hearers, the preachers of the seventeenth and eighteenth centuries occasionally produced versifications of their sermons. These could scarcely be called poetry, but their rhythm and rhyme greatly assisted in the retention of the truth. The Scotsman Ralph Erskine produced a rhyme of this sort in which he indicated the Puritan views on the place of the law in the believer's life. Here is part of that sonnet of 386 verses, which he entitled "The Believer's Principles Concerning the Law and the Gospel":

> *The law's a tutor much in vogue,*
> *To gospel-grace a pedagogue;*
> *The gospel to the law no less*
> *Than its full end for righteousness.*
>
> *When once the fiery law of God*
> *Has chas'd me to the gospel-road;*
> *Then back unto the holy law*
> *Most kindly gospel-grace will draw.*

When by the law to grace I'm schooled;
Grace by the law will have me ruled;
Hence, if I don't the law obey,
I cannot keep the gospel-way.

When I the gospel-news believe,
Obedience to the law I give;
And that both in its fed'ral dress,
And as a rule of holiness.

What in the gospel-mint is coined,
The same is in the law enjoined:
Whatever gospel-tidings teach,
The law's authority doth reach.

Here join the law and gospel hands,
What this me teaches that commands:
What virtuous forms the gospel please
The same the law doth authorise.

And thus the law-commandment seals
Whatever gospel-grace reveals:
The gospel also for my good
Seals all the law-demands with blood.

The law most perfect still remains,
And every duty full contains:
The gospel its perfection speaks,
And therefore gives whate'er it seeks.

Law-threats and precepts both, I see,
With gospel-promises agree;
They to the gospel are a fence,
And it to them a maintenance.

The law will justify all those
Who with the gospel-ransom close;

The gospel too approves for aye
All those that do the law obey.

A rigid master was the law,
Demanding brick, denying straw;
But when with gospel-tongue it sings,
It bids me fly, and gives me wings.

In this paradox lies the perfect wisdom of God. The appropriate prayer of the true believer may well be that of the psalmist, "Give me understanding, and I shall keep Your law; indeed I shall observe it with my whole heart" (Ps. 119:34).

THE GOSPEL IS, INDEED, OUR TRUST—bountiful blessings inherited through God's grace. As trustee of this estate, we are obligated to ensure its preservation for future generations. That responsibility demands that we preserve the relationship between the law and the gospel, showing in our lives how they mutually serve and establish one another.

APPENDIX A

Calvin on the Covenant

THE FOLLOWING IS FROM THE INTRODUCTION to John Calvin's *Tracts and Treatises on the Reformation of the Church* (Grand Rapids: Eerdmans, 1958), 1:xxi-xxiii.

For Calvin the Covenant represented the gracious and eternal will of God to ally Himself with His creatures as their God and Saviour, to commit Himself to His people in paternal kindness, and to take them into communion with Himself as His dear children. Calvin took the form of this Covenant to be expressed in the words: "I will be your God, and you shall be my people." This Covenant is as old as creation, but it was when God said specifically to Abraham, "I will be a God to you and to your seed after you," that the Church was separated out from the nations and brought into definite being as the divinely appointed sphere in history of God's revealing and redeeming activity.

In this Covenant God declared His will for His people: "I am your God. Walk before me and be perfect. I am holy; therefore be ye holy." This Covenant was sealed with two major Sacraments: circumcision, which inscribed the promise of God's blessing in the flesh of his people and covenanted them to a life of obedience and faith; and the passover in which God renewed His Covenant promising His people redemption from the bondage of sin and the tyranny of the powers of evil into fellowship with Himself through a sacrifice which God Himself would provide. This Covenant was thus essentially a Covenant of grace. God knew that His people would be unable to keep the Covenant, and to walk before Him in obedience to His holy Will, and so in His paternal kindness and mercy He provided within the Covenant a way of obedient response to His loving-kindness, and a way of cleansing and restoration to fellowship with Himself. Not only, therefore, did He give His people His Word and Sacraments through which He revealed Himself familiarly to them and adopted them as His children, but He provided for them a Law which clearly set forth His Will, and an order of worship and sacrifice in the Cult [the word "Cult" meaning something quite different than it does today] which supplied His people in their weakness with a covenanted way of response to His Will. Both of these were also a testimony to the fact that mercy and judgment belonged to God alone. Calvin insisted that the Old Testament Cult and Law belong inseparably together, and that if divorced from the Law the Cult has no meaning; it functions only within the sphere of God's Covenant-will as a testimony to His holiness, and as a sign and promise of His reconciling mercy. Moreover, the Cult and the Priesthood were designed to educate God's people by means of ceremonies into a true understanding of sin and forgiveness, to lead them into the way of obedience, and to hold constantly before them the promise of Messianic salvation.

That is the Covenant of the Old Testament, and it is the same as the Covenant of the New Testament. There is only one Covenant, but between the Old and the New Testaments there is a difference in *economy* or *administration*. The *substance* of the Covenant remains the same, although in the old economy it was given under the form of promise, and in the new economy it is fulfilled in Christ, so that in the New Testament we have a more "solid participation" in the substance of the Covenant than in the Old. Even here the essential form of the Covenant remains the same, for here too the Covenant has two essential parts: a declaration of gratuitous love to which was annexed the promise of a blessed life, and a sincere endeavor to walk before God in faith and holiness. But here too, and here above all, God in His great mercy provides us with a covenanted way of response to His Will in the obedience and sacrifice of Jesus Christ, in whom the old form of the Covenant is completely fulfilled.

According to Calvin the change in the economy or administration of the Covenant began to take place under the teaching of the great prophets, particularly, Isaiah, Jeremiah, and Ezekiel, while the first beginnings of the Church in the New Testament sense are to be discerned in the return of the remnant from the Babylonian exile. This change Calvin saw to be focussed around the concept of the Servant of the Lord who fulfilled in His own body and soul the Covenant-will of God for his people, and who fulfilled also the covenanted obedience of the people to God's holy Will. This righteous Servant, described in the book of Isaiah, was Christ, so that already in the midst of the Old Covenant the clear message of the New was being set forth. Thus of Isaiah 53:11 Calvin said: "He shews that Christ justifies us, not only as He is God, but also as He is man; for in our flesh He procured righteousness for us. He does not say 'the Son,' but 'my Servant,' that we may not only view Him as God, but may contemplate His human nature, in which He performed that obedience by which we are acquitted before God. The foundation of our salvation is this, that he offered Himself a sacrifice, and in like manner, He Himself declares, 'For their sakes I sanctify Myself, that they also may be holy.'" Christ is thus the substance of both forms of the one Covenant. In the Old Covenant He was offered in a promise that was to be fulfilled in the future; and in the New Covenant he is offered as the One in whom all the promises have already been realized.

Corresponding to this change in the economy of the Covenant there were changes in regard to doctrine and worship that must be noted, for they are of the utmost significance.

The Covenant is fulfilled in Christ, the Covenant-union with God is fulfilled in communion with Christ through the Spirit; that is to say, it is fulfilled in the Church as the Body of Christ. This union with Christ is of the very essence of the New Covenant, and for this reason personal and sacramental communion with Christ transcended the form of union with God under ceremony and law.

APPENDIX B

For Further Reading

ANYONE SEEKING A TRUE UNDERSTANDING of the law and gospel would do well to study the following passages from the letters of the apostle Paul:

2 Corinthians 3:2–18	Romans 5:12–21
Galatians 2:14–21	Romans 6:14–18
Galatians 3:19–26	Romans 7
Galatians 4:1–7	Romans 10:4–9
Galatians 5:13–15	Romans 14:1–7
Romans 2:13–15	Ephesians 2:11–17
Romans 3:19–20	Colossians 2:11–17
Romans 3:31	1 Timothy 1:6–11

It would be beyond the scope of this book to address all of these texts. But they receive careful exposition in Patrick Fairbairn's *The Revelation of Law in Scripture* (reprint: Phillipsburg, N.J.: P&R Publishing, 1996), 365-480.

Also beyond the scope of this book (and certainly beyond my theological qualifications) is another closely related subject, the covenants. That subject is so important in relation to the law and the gospel that Spurgeon considered the covenant the marrow of divinity. (See also Appendix A: Calvin on the Covenant.)

Four books that I enthusiastically recommend as the best on the subject of the covenants are:

1. Herman Witsius, *The Economy of the Covenants Between God and Man*, 2 vols.

195

2. O. Palmer Robertson, *The Christ of the Covenants*.
3. Francis Turretin, *Institutes of Elenctic Theology, vol. 2*.
4. Zacharias Ursinus, *Commentary on the Heidelberg Catechism*.

Each of these four titles has been published or reissued by P&R Publishing and may be purchased from them.